Cambridge Elements ☰

Elements in Publishing and Book Culture
edited by
Samantha Rayner
University College London
Leah Tether
University of Bristol

THE SPACES OF BOOKSELLING

Stores, Streets, and Pages

Kristen Doyle Highland
American University of Sharjah

CAMBRIDGE
UNIVERSITY PRESS

Shaftesbury Road, Cambridge CB2 8EA, United Kingdom

One Liberty Plaza, 20th Floor, New York, NY 10006, USA

477 Williamstown Road, Port Melbourne, VIC 3207, Australia

314–321, 3rd Floor, Plot 3, Splendor Forum, Jasola District Centre,
New Delhi – 110025, India

103 Penang Road, #05–06/07, Visioncrest Commercial, Singapore 238467

Cambridge University Press is part of Cambridge University Press & Assessment,
a department of the University of Cambridge.

We share the University's mission to contribute to society through the pursuit of
education, learning and research at the highest international levels of excellence.

www.cambridge.org
Information on this title: cambridge.org/9781108822886

DOI: 10.1017/9781108906500

First published 2023

A catalogue record for this publication is available from the British Library.

ISBN 978-1-108-82288-6 Paperback
ISSN 2514-8524 (online)
ISSN 2514-8516 (print)

The Spaces of Bookselling

Stores, Streets, and Pages

Elements in Publishing and Book Culture

DOI: 10.1017/9781108906500
First published online: February 2023

Kristen Doyle Highland
American University of Sharjah

Author for correspondence: Kristen Doyle Highland, khighland@aus.edu

ABSTRACT: The spaces of bookselling have as many stories to tell as do the books for sale. More than static backgrounds for bookselling, these dynamic spaces both shape individual and collective behaviors and perceptions and are shaped by the values and practices of booksellers and book buyers. This Element focuses primarily on bookselling in the United States from the nineteenth through the twenty-first centuries and examines three key bookselling spaces – the store, the street, and the catalogue. Following an introduction, the second section considers how the material space of bookstores shapes social engagement in and cultural values associated with the bookstore. The third section turns to itinerant and sidewalk booksellers and the ways in which they use the physical, social, and legal space of the street to craft geographies of belonging. And the final section pages through bookseller catalogues, examining them as a significant genre that works to spatialize the bookstore.

KEYWORDS: bookselling, bookstore, space, community, book history

ISBNs: 9781108822886 (PB), 9781108906500 (OC)
ISSNs: 2514-8524 (online), 2514-8516 (print)

Contents

1 Introduction

1.1 Siting Bookselling

Site: Stores

After an afternoon visit to D. Appleton & Co's bookstore in early November 1836, sixteen-year-old New Yorker George Templeton Strong sat down to his diary. The future lawyer, bibliophile, and founder of Columbia Law School remarked on recent renovations to the store at 200 Broadway:

> [Appleton] has had his store expanded so that the Old Books, instead of being literally crammed upstairs, will be provided with some sort of decent accommodations below. It is a very good plan, for they were afraid the floor would break through, and moreover it was scarcely possible to navigate upstairs for the folios that were heaped up in piles six or eight feet high.[1]

Site: Streets

The passage of Local Law 45 in New York City in 1993 restricted the spaces for sidewalk book and magazine vending. Following the passage of this law, Hakim Hasan, a Black sidewalk bookseller, described to sociologist and collaborator Mitchell Duneier his experience setting up his table near a gourmet grocery store:

> Yesterday I came into New York and set up twenty feet from the entrance to Balducci's Supermarket and ten feet from the intersection.
>
> There is no where else to work right now.
>
> I knew that, if necessary, I was going to set up on the block where Balducci's is located a long time ago. I never

---

[1] Strong, "Nov 3, 1836" in *The Diary*, 41.

told anyone that I studied the location and placement logistics for every block in the Village. [. . .]

Within ten minutes a Puerto Rican Balducci's security guard with a cheap "March of the Wooden Soldiers" uniform says to me, "I am just trying to be nice. You can't stay here. You gotta leave."

"This is public space," I told him. "This is a *legal* location for vending. I do not want to be here, but I can't work down the street. So, you are gonna have to call the police."

Anyway the police come in an unmarked wine red car. Two patrol officers and the Sergeant in the back seat.

The tape measure comes out.

Are you ten feet from the intersection?

I'm more than ten feet and I'm twenty feet from the entrance to their store. [. . .]

One of the patrol officers says to me, "You know the law pretty well, huh?" [. . .]

The sergeant had to get back in her car and leave. They *cannot* move me. They have no *legal basis* to move me without running the risk of being *sued*. She knows this.[2]

Site: Pages

In 2003, Loompanics released their latest book catalogue. The bookseller, self-described as specializing in "the lunatic fringe of the libertarian movement," included thirty-five separate subject categories in the 286-page catalogue, including such subjects as "Privacy and Hiding Things," "Head for the Hills," and "Paralegal Skills." The introduction pages introduce the catalogue:

Herein you will find controversial and unusual books on a wide variety of subjects. Most of these books cannot be found in even the largest libraries. The majority of them will

[2] Qtd in Duneier, *Sidewalk*, 277–278.

never be seen in bookstores. They are *here* now – available
to you.[3]

1.2 Space and Bookselling

We know retail bookselling to be a multifaceted economic, political, and
social practice. What the above vignettes remind us is that bookselling is
also a spatial practice. It happens in stores, along streets and sidewalks, and
in the pages of catalogues and newspapers. More than flat settings or static
stages upon which booksellers, customers, and readers engage, these spatial
mediums act, shaping individual and collective behaviors, associations, and
meanings. And in turn, bookselling acts on spaces, refiguring values and
practices associated with community and belonging and leisure and reading.
"It's not just what we do but where we do it," argues Mark Paterson in
Consumption and Everyday Life, "so that the spatial contexts of cultural
practices often help structure the activities occurring within them."[4] So how
do we locate and create an archive of bookselling spaces? How do we make
sense of the means through which these spaces are shaping or being shaped
by the dynamics of bookselling? This element explores the ways in which
bookselling accumulates and creates layered meanings through its spatial
contexts, including the built environment and design of stores, the social
space and boundaries of the street, and amid the paratextual covers and lists
in the bookseller's catalogue. It understands bookselling spaces as social,
collective, created, and contingent.

To help elucidate these spatial dimensions, each section in this element
draws on diverse conceptualizations of space as articulated by a number of
prominent spatial theorists, including Henri Lefebvre, Michel de Certeau,
Doreen Massey, Edward Soja, and Tim Cresswell.[5] In addition, the analyses of material, social, and discursive spaces are informed by the work of
scholars across a range of fields, from architecture and urban studies, to

---

[3] Loompanics, *2003 The Best Book Catalog/*.

[4] Paterson, *Consumption and Everyday Life*, 171.

[5] Lefebvre, *The Production of Space*; de Certeau, *The Practice of Everyday Life*;
Massey, *Space, Place, and Gender*; Soja, *Third Space*; Cresswell, *On the Move*.

cultural geography and sociology, to media and literary studies. While these diverse theorists and scholars offer a variety of ways to conceptualize and "read" space, they are unified by the assertion that space is constructed socially, politically, and phenomenologically.

This element is also in conversation with work in book history, literary studies, and history that considers the spatial dimensions of books and print. Historian Adrian Johns has argued that we must "look to the hard, continuous work of real people in real places," paying attention to "particular streets, buildings, floors, and rooms" to understand how the abstract concept of print culture was given specific form and meaning.[6] Increasing attention to spatiality and geographies of the book have resulted in analyses focused on the movement of books through space, the "bookscapes" of seventeenth- and eighteenth-century London, and the spatial arrangement of stock and contemporary standardized store design, for example.[7] In addition, institutional histories such as Abigail Van Slyck on the Carnegie Libraries in early-twentieth-century America and Thomas Augst and Kenneth Carpenter's analysis of the social life of American libraries stress the ways in which physical library spaces are socially, culturally, and ideologically significant.[8] And finally, the field of historical GIS highlights how spatial relationships of proximity and movement support larger social and economic networks.[9]

This element expands and deepens the essential and growing interest in how space and bookselling function in dynamic relation. An attention to spatial dynamics – as opposed to economics or literary import – broadens the questions we ask (and the insights we might glean) concerning the cultural and social work of bookselling and the material places we look to discern this work. By making spatiality the interpretive compass, we might

[6] Johns, *Nature of the Book*, 42.

[7] Ogborn and Withers, *Geographies of the Book;* Raven, *Bookscape*; Zboray, *A Fictive People*, Ch. 6; Miller, *Reluctant Capitalists*, Ch. 4.

[8] Van Slyck, *Free to All*; Augst and Carpenter, *Institutions of Reading*.

[9] See, for instance, Black, Martin, and MacDonald, "Geographic Information Systems"; Smith, "Space"; Zboray and Zboray, "The Boston Booktrades"; Highland, "In the Bookstore".

cross traditional boundaries that tend to separate discussions of bookselling by specific sale method or that focus on singular booksellers. Instead, a focus on the spaces of bookselling – bringing together bookstore, itinerant bookselling, sidewalk bookselling, and the mail-order catalogue – bridges formal and informal economies, the material environment and the material page, and physical distance and social spaces, expanding our understanding of the complex layered geographies of bookselling.

In addition, and important in our current era of both increasing connection and deepening division, by studying the spatiality of bookselling, we gain a deeper understanding of the ways in which bookselling operates within and shapes larger social and cultural patterns related to race and gender and community and belonging. How do we understand the lived experiences of diverse individuals? How do we forge connection and community life? How are power and status negotiated in the spaces we share? These questions are all central to scholars who study spatiality, and bookselling spaces offer a rich – and essential – medium for exploring these questions anew. Urban studies, for instance, has long been interested in street commerce, but does not often distinguish between street booksellers and other types of vending. Although they are regular vendors, street booksellers are also distinctive by virtue of the products they sell – books. Located in a liminal space between the cultural and commercial, books are more than physical goods. And booksellers sell more than books. They sell stories about how and why and what we read, stories about the ways in which (and where) we engage with and understand one another, and stories about who we think we are as individuals and collectives.

To begin to tell these stories, this element focuses primarily on bookselling in the United States from the eighteenth to the twenty-first centuries. The second section, "Stores: Constructing Meaning in the Bookstore," offers a broader, though necessarily selective geography, roaming across Europe, the Middle East, Asia, and Africa. This section examines how the material space of bookstores – focusing specifically on the built environment and the spatial logics of stock organization – shapes ideas and practices of reading, identity, knowledge, and community, and, in return, how booksellers and book buyers reshape and reinscribe the bookstore with diverse cultural meanings and purposes.

Section three exits the bookstore onto the streets and sidewalks. "Streets: Books, Boundaries, and Belonging" explores the street and sidewalk as dynamic spaces for navigating, transgressing, and redrawing gendered and racialized boundaries of belonging for the bookseller and their customers. Drawing on concepts of the social production of space outlined by Lefebvre, Soja, and others, this section highlights the political potential for transformation through itinerant and sidewalk bookselling.

The final section, "Pages: Navigating Bookseller Catalogues," turns to the booksellers catalogue. Although catalogues are most often valued as repositories of bibliographic information, I argue here that they should be read as a dynamic spatial and spatializing genre. Drawing together concepts of the paratext, urban wayfinding, and Joanna Drucker's "phenomenal book," I show how a reader's interaction with structural elements of the catalogue actively creates the meaningful space of the bookstore, guiding readers through real and imagined space and shaping values and practices associated with reading and knowledge production.[10]

Through diverse forms of evidence, from memoirs to news articles to city ordinances to advocacy publications, among others, this element offers multiple vistas for viewing, narrating, and analyzing bookselling spaces. Of course, in a minigraph-sized publication, one's surveying eye must necessarily be limited. Indeed, I make no claim to comprehensiveness. The metaphor of wayfinding invoked in the fourth section to analyze the spatial work of bookseller catalogues can also be considered a methodological practice in which the researcher acknowledges and embraces the necessarily selective process of research and writing. As one wayfinds in the physical world through paying attention to specific landmarks and ignoring others, the researcher focuses on some examples to the exclusion of many more. It is my hope that this element serves as an invitation to continue expanding our study of bookselling and its forms and spaces in all of their diversity.

[10] Drucker, "The Virtual Codex," para. 14.

2 Stores: Constructing Meaning in the Bookstore

In November 2020, amid the cascading economic and social crises of the COVID pandemic, graphic-novel publisher SelfMadeHero announced a Twitter campaign to benefit the shuttered doors of independent bookstores. #DrawYourBookshop asked participants to contribute "a quick sketch, drawing, or masterpiece" of their favorite local bookstore.[11] Aligning bookstores with other cultural institutions like theaters, concert halls, and art galleries, the campaign sought to "rebrand our bookshops as an essential service and recognize the existential crisis they are facing."

Hundreds of people across the globe responded to the call, submitting pencil, ink, and colored illustrations of their favorite bookstores. Many images feature prominently named storefronts with warmly lit interiors and lively window displays. Rain or snow added atmosphere. Other illustrations privilege people – children eagerly peering at colorful covers through the window or neighbors exchanging books with one another just outside the doors of the shop. And a few offer a glimpse of cozy, book-crowded interiors.[12] Like the trade cards of the nineteenth century, the bookstores are insistently emplaced in their locality by their prominent store names while also divorced from all other contexts. The bookshop front appears like a single book cover, disconnected from the surrounding shops, the street, or even its geographic location. It is the facade of the bookstore itself, its two-dimensional image on the page, in which meaning inheres. The goal of the campaign was both specific – your favorite bookstore – and abstract – one bookstore stands for ALL bookstores. In these images, it is the interplay between the local and universal and the material and symbolic that provides the dimensionality of meaning to the viewers. Bookstores are given meaning through intensely local relationships as well as through their abstract symbolic connection to culture and community.

---

[11] "#DrawYourBookshop," *Self-Made Hero Graphic Novels Visual Narratives*, November 16, 2020. www.selfmadehero.com/news/drawyourbookshop. Original tweet: https://twitter.com/SelfMadeHero/status/1328603825264005124.

[12] Browse #DrawYourBookshop entries by searching the hashtag on Twitter.

Discourse around the cultural significance of the bookstore can become flattened in the false binary between commerce and culture. Is the bookstore primarily a business? Or is the bookstore a cultural institution? Of course, it is both. As scholar Huw Osborne has noted, "bookshops have long operated within the fraught space formed" by the "twinned and competing forces" of commerce and culture.[13] It's the very inextricability of commerce as culture and culture as commerce that endows the bookstore with such resonance. The description of the #DrawYourBookshop campaign recognizes that the economic wellbeing of the bookstore is bound to its existential meaning. We can buy books from a number of outlets, but the cultural value of the brick-and-mortar bookstore compels us to buy books there. The bookstore must both move books and anchor community. The individual and collective values ascribed to and framed by bookstores are found in these overlapping and shifting layers of the economic, social, political, and imaginative. The spatial and material contexts of the bookstore ground these layers. The axes of the built environment of the bookstore – the drawn lines of the façade of the storefront, its horizontal rows and aisles, its vertical shelving, the horizon of its single floor or the stacked subterranean and upper floors – shape forms and patterns of consumer and social practices. Within these spaces we plot our own material and symbolic meanings and in so doing, create, negotiate, and change the space of the bookstore.

This section moves among these layers of the economic, social, political, and imaginative by focusing on how the built environment of the store and the interior spatial organization of its shelves and stock inform meanings associated with the bookstore. The first subsection traces two dominant typologies of the bookstore, the intimate and the monumental, in order to discern how these forms shape the complex social purposes and symbolic associations of the bookstore. Then the section turns to the internal organization of shelving and stock arrangement to track the link between the spatial logics of organization and constructions of knowledge and identity. Overall, I hope to emphasize how the material spaces of the bookstore embody symbolic values and associations that ultimately transcend the

---

[13] Osborne, "Introduction: Openings," 1.

physical store and imbue "the bookstore" with such powerful cultural resonance.

2.1 Typologies: The Intimate and the Monumental

In describing its welcoming aspect, the website of well-known Denver, Colorado, bookstore Tattered Cover explains that the store features "lots of nooks & crannies that offer the intimacy and comfort of smaller bookshops."[14] Novelist Elin Hilderbrand celebrates her favorite bookstore, Bookworks in Nantucket, Massachusetts, as "cozy and not unlike a rabbit warren – shelves and shelves of books, nooks and crannies, places to sit."[15] When, in 2014, longtime London bookseller chain Foyles embarked on a massive remodel of the former Central Saint Martin's Art School to house their new flagship store on Charing Cross Road, customers were worried. As chairman Christopher Foyle explained, they "were concerned that we were going to do away with all the nooks and crannies and make it too modern."[16] Nooks and crannies – an out-of-the-way corner, those small spaces in which we both lose and find ourselves. A discovered space of physical and psychological intimacy in the midst of the public store. A hidden space that hides from the ubiquitous monitoring of modernity.[17]

That the "nook and cranny" motif is so often evoked in the context of the bookstore highlights both a dominant spatial typology of the bookstore and a conceptualization of the role of the bookstore as an intimate domesticized retreat removed from the insistent demands of modern time. Counter to the demands of the day and the modes of modernity, the corners of bookstores invite slowing, stillness, and seclusion. Nooks, niches,

---

[14] "Tattered History."

[15] Hilderbrand, *My Bookstore*, 153. Writers have also, of course, crafted fictional bookstores in their works. On these "bookstore novels," see Muse, *Fantasies of the Bookstore*.

[16] Campbell, "Foyles' New Flagship."

[17] The spatialized metaphor of the nook is also invoked in its perceived opposite – the "big box" bookstore. The box is an overly open, undifferentiated space and (too simplistically) a homogenized experience. Yet, the nook persists: Barnes and Noble's branded e-reader is The Nook.

crannies, and corners all call on Gaston Bachelard's spatial theorizations. In *Poetics of Space*, he explains, "the corner is a haven that ensures us one of the things we prize most highly – immobility."[18] Immobility. Stillness. The individual pauses in that cranny or corner. Time itself pauses. "An imaginary room rises around our bodies," Bachelard continues, "which think that they are well hidden when we take refuge in a corner."[19] The corners and nooks and crannies so prominent in bookstore design and descriptions serve as individual and societal refuges. The fear of losing nooks and crannies to a "too modern" space is to fear this loss of individual and collective refuge, of the ability to exist alone with oneself, to still time. Of course, the size of bookstores is also a product of the logistics of available real estate and the economic constraints of rent and retail profits. However, while the pressures of capitalism might mold the corners of bookstores, the symbolic space of the intimate bookstore – its nooks and crannies, its coziness – acts as a material and figurative bulwark against these same forces.

The "corner" as immobile, as haven, is also called to mind in the corner store. New York and Boston each host a famous Corner Bookstore. Innumerable other cities and towns from Beaverton, Oregon, to Halifax, West Yorkshire, to Johannesburg, South Africa, to Dubai in the United Arab Emirates have a Book Corner or Corner Books or even a Globe Corner Bookstore. The corner store, whether invoked in the name or by its physical location, embodies and preserves the intimacy of home and neighborhood. The Three Lives Bookstore in the West Village in New York City is physically located on a corner, and it's the symbolic dimensions of the corner store that informs owner Toby Cox's connection with the shop: "I loved the idea of a corner bookshop. It was part of what the Village always meant – a little bit of civility and a welcoming face, a place where people buy books and sometimes neighbors leave their keys."[20] The corner shop preserves the "always meant," the idealized identity of a neighborhood; it resists change; it remains familiar, welcoming, intimate.

The intimate space of the corner or the corner shop invokes ideas of home as a physical and figurative space. Bachelard notes that the corner,

---

[18] Bachelard, *The Poetics of Space*, 137. [19] Ibid.

[20] Nadelson, "In Greenwich Village."

that "secluded space" of hiddenness or personal withdrawal, "is the germ of a room, or of a house."[21] Certainly, bookstores have long maintained an associative corollary with the home. The overstuffed chairs, couches, piled books, and lamp lighting that inform romantic visuals of the ideal bookstore gesture toward the living room and a rich domestic life. For writer and cultural critic Jorge Carrión, the "large wooden tables and sofa and a basement with rugs" at the Book Lounge in Johannesburg, South Africa, "makes you want to stay on and live there."[22] Bookstores have been productively discussed within sociologists Ray Oldenburg and Dennis Brissett's conception of third place, which imagines bookstores and similar social environments to be neither home nor work, but rather alternative public places that facilitate community identity and social and creative interactions.[23] But Carrión's characterization of bookstores as "momentary homes" gets closer to locating the symbolic power of the typology of the intimate bookstore.[24] In the spatial and symbolic conception of the bookstore as a domestic space animated by its nooks and crannies and corners and thus resistant to the physical and temporal demands of modern society, the bookstore is more home than home. It is the ideal home.

For Pages Bookstore in Istanbul, Turkey, this material and symbolic link between the bookstore and home assumes added resonance for a refugee population. The tagline of the Arabic language bookstore, founded by Syrian publishers and refugees Samar Al-Kadri and his wife, Gulnar Hajo, is "Pages, it's your home."[25] The store is both a literal and a figurative home. Occupying a three-story greenwood-sided house in a residential neighborhood of Istanbul, Pages provides a connection to the home countries of displaced Syrians, Iraqis, and Yemenis.[26] One child customer explained of his experience in the store, "I felt like I was in Syria with all these Arabic books."[27] As a confluence of public policy, immigration law, political ethnonationalism, and socioeconomic difference conspire to make them strangers in Turkey, displaced individuals sit at the small

[21] Bachelard, *Poetics of Space*, 136. [22] Carrión, *Bookshops*, 215.

[23] Oldenburg and Brissett, "The Third Place." [24] Carrión, *Bookshops*, 62.

[25] *Pages Bookstore Café Istanbul*. [26] Arango, "Syrian Migrants in Istanbul."

[27] Shaheen, "Istanbul Bookshop."

wooden tables and upholstered armchairs amid the exposed brick, built-in bookshelves, curtained windows, and dim floor lamps in the front living room/café of Pages Bookstore and debate whether to go home or to make a new home. The domestic space of the bookstore provides a safe house, a refuge for a community to examine and enact complicated relationships to their own experiences and ideas of home.

As evinced by Pages Bookstore, home as a material space is political. The invocation of tropes of intimacy and home in the bookstore is about more than comfort and familiarity; these forms can also provide space to assert political agency. In astute design decisions, many activist and movement-oriented bookstores draw on the materialities and connotations of home to extend the political salience of domestic spaces into the bookstore.[28] For the displaced in Al-Kadri's Istanbul store, the location of the bookstore in a residential neighborhood claims a house and permanence for a transitory community. The café is located in what would be the living room or salon of the home, offering spatial encouragement for conversation and storytelling, and to build community and the foundations of advocacy. In *The New Women's Survival Catalog*, published in 1973 to document feminist cultural activity and activism in the United States, images of feminist bookstores spotlight domestic elements. In one bookstore, a woman reads on a tapestry-covered oversize armchair beside a self-service metal coffee machine; another sits alone by a large shaded window in a sectioned-off living room space complete with couch, bucket chair, coffee table, and house plant.[29] No book stacks, that core element of a bookstore, are visible in either image. In the former home of Austin, Texas', Resistencia Books, dedicated to supporting the art and culture of the Indigenous, Chicano/a, and Latino/a communities, a room features framed wall art, handmade area rugs on wood floors, and wallpaper-lined bookcases containing art, pottery, crafts, books, and pictures, calling to mind the diverse personal contents of bookcases in homes. Vases, some with artificial flowers, dot the room. Wainscoting along the wall, an attic access, and

---

[28] Kinder, *The Radical Bookstore*, 25. Kinder also labels these stores "print-based movement spaces" (29).

[29] Grimstad and Rennie, *The New Woman's Survival Catalog*, 22–23.

a ceiling fan further domesticate the space. This intentional design draws on and reimbues the political potential of home spaces within the bookstore. In this room in Resistencia, Latino/a collectives and socialist groups meet and organize and high school students of color learn about activist literature.[30] As the store has become a communal space for the LGBTQ community and artists and writers of color, bookstore volunteer and community advocate Bianca Flores explains, "we like to think of this place as another home for people."[31]

Home is also a salient spatial form and metaphor for black-owned bookstores. American author and activist bell hooks describes "homeplace" as a process of claiming space outside of the repressive contexts of racism and white supremacy. For Black women, in particular, hooks notes, home-place is a private and subversive space: "Domestic space has been a crucial site for organizing, for forming political solidarity. Homeplace has been a site of resistance."[32] Historian Shannon King further notes that the political power of residential spaces was important for the Black community "because it allowed blacks to take back and, sometimes, remake places of 'congregation' or what we now call 'safe spaces.'"[33] As Black-owned book-stores proliferated in America and Britain during the Black Power move-ment to serve a "growing appetite for books by and about black people," and as their numbers have grown again amid continuing contexts of injustice, they have adapted these concepts of home, community, and congregation within physical stores.[34] For instance, in Sister's Uptown Bookstore and Community Center in Harlem, New York, displayed art and textiles from African and local African-American artists invoke com-munity and kinship. With bookshelves lining the perimeter walls, the open center floor makes space for African folk heritage circles, book clubs, and community events.[35] As writer Edwidge Danticat has noted, Black book-stores "are more than bookstores. They're places of community-building; they're places of fellowship."[36]

---

[30] Kinder, *The Radical Bookstore*, 25–27.

[31] Hamilton, "Casa de Resistancia Bookstore." [32] hooks, *Yearning*, 47.

[33] Blain, "Community Politics." [34] Davis, "The FBI's War."

[35] Kravitz, "Sisters Uptown Bookstore." [36] Connor, "Brooklyn's Nkiru Books."

THE WOMEN'S STORE
4157 Adams Street, San Diego, California

SISTERHOOD BOOKSTORE

Like most women's bookstores, SISTERHOOD is more than just a bookstore. It is an exquisitely-designed environment which has, in addition to an excellent range of titles, feminist-made posters, jewelry, pottery, and art. There is a comfortable reading nook equipped with a coffee machine and a bulletin board which keeps customers informed of feminist activities around town.

In the short period of its existence (1½ years), SISTERHOOD has had to move twice to deal with expansion. But success is no secret in this case, as SISTERHOOD is clearly one of the most beautiful and friendly bookstores you'll ever come across.

1351 Westwood Boulevard
Los Angeles, California 90024
(213) 477-7300

22

Figure 1 *The New Woman's Survival Catalog*, edited by Kirsten Grimstad and Susan Rennie (1973/2019). Courtesy of Kirsten Grimstad, Susan Rennie, and Primary Information.

Information Center Incorporated

A

Woman's

Place

"As women come together in the growth of the women's movement, as women got interested in mingling with other women, it became clear that there was no place we could go and not be interfered with by men. No place to socialize in, no place to hang out. Well, there were laundromats, beauty parlors, and gay bars. Laundromats and beauty parlors just don't make it. We're tired gay bars and let's face it, they don't make it either, for a variety of reasons we won't go into here, for a variety of reasons.

"A group of us have gotten together and opened a bookstore. We call it ICI—A Woman's Place Bookstore. The ICI stands for Information Center Incorporate.

"This bookstore is different from most bookstores. It has tables and chairs to sit and relax at, and coffee and tea and nibbles. There are bulletin boards that women can use to get in touch with other women. And of course, a bookstore run by feminists is different from a bookstore with a feminist section in it. The store is a pretty good size, so we can have regular rap groups, poetry readings, movies, etc. . . .

"Energy and information are interrelated. The receiving and transmitting of information, especially the kinds that woman-identified-women see looking for, is one of our top priorities. On the one hand, we push written information. On the other hand, we believe that revolutionary re-forming change comes through person-to-person contact. Each such hand will wash the other, so to speak. We do not believe in EITHER this OR that; we believe in both this AND that."

A WOMAN'S PLACE was opened in January, 1972 by a collective of six women, now grown to eleven. All put in time in the store without pay, supporting themselves with other full- or part-time jobs. This does not imply a belief in volunteerism; the women look eventually to supporting themselves from the bookstore; but, at the present time, they see building the store's stock as their chief priority.

This policy has been very fruitful. Starting with four bookshelves, A WOMAN'S PLACE is today the largest, best-stocked feminist bookstore in the United States. Only SISTERHOOD BOOKSTORE in Los Angeles offers a comparable variety of books, pamphlets, magazines, newspapers, posters. The poetry collection is exceptional. This may be partly because the store shares space with the OAKLAND WOMEN'S PRESS COLLECTIVE (see PRESSES), which prints and publishes outstanding women's poetry. The store also carries a wide range of hard-to-find feminist pamphlets.

A WOMAN'S PLACE occupies a very large, very comfortable space. There are indeed "tables and chairs to sit and relax at." Also, a bulletin board that most total at least twenty by eight feet. Very little goes on in the Bay area women's movement that is not posted here. As Alice confided to us, "A WOMAN'S PLACE is really a Women's Center disguised as a bookstore." Some disguise.

Write to:

A WOMAN'S PLACE
5251 Broadway
Oakland, California 94618
(415) 654-9920

STARTING A BOOKSTORE:
Non-Capitalist Operation within
a Capitalist Economy

"How do you decide what can be done with the available funds. You sit down and do some very realistic figuring. In addition to the cost of merchandise there are basic inescapable expenses to be met monthly and a few annual or semi-annual expenses for which you have to be prepared. Each locality varies, so you must work these out for yourself, but I list the most probable with some suggestions on how to meet them.

"How can you know the true cost of sales? You can't very well figure item by item. It requires keeping an inventory record of the cost in its relationship to the retail price. It means keep and summarize all those nasty little pieces of immaterable size and shape and design. With this % applied to Sales and the result reduced by that adjusted overhead figure, you have a pretty accurate figure on which to ponder. Only at year end when you do a physical count of the actual inventory left, do you put this into the ledger and know for sure what the answer really is. See why I say it takes long-term commitment?

"With the rapidly growing disillusionment with big business and capitalism in general, we feel our experiment is a transition: toward a more equitable form of the future, comparable to the various forms of cooperatives. Such a future would be one where each individual earned the needs of the community according to ability and personal interest and thereby qualified for a reasonable share, small but adequate food, shelter, clothing, but without interest in or ambition toward personal accumulation of wealth and useless possessions."

These are excerpts from an informal letter of advice on how to start a women's bookstore. It is filled with invaluable nuts-and-bolts suggestions, and certainly would help inexperienced women decide whether to launch such a venture. The women at ICI are willing to share this information with other feminists who wish to start a bookstore.

Write to:

ICI—A Woman's Place
5251 Broadway
Oakland, California 94618

Send 25¢ to cover costs of reproduction
and postage.

23

Figure 1 (Cont.)

The bookstore as a domestic space, with its stuffed chairs and couches impersonating living rooms and its hidden nooks and corners, looms large in cultural conceptions of the bookstore. It seeps into our historical imagination as well. Indeed, so strong is the imaginative power of this intimate and sheltered spatial dynamic that historian James Raven, in his meticulous examination of floorplans, tax receipts, and fire records of London bookshops and print houses before 1800, notes that scholarly studies, including a few of his own, have "tended to exaggerate the hunched, narrow, tall, and compact character" of these stores.[37]

A turn to another bookseller in the past offers an introduction to an alternative typology of the bookstore, grander in scale and design though equally as evocative. In 1854, the New York City press celebrated the move of bookseller Daniel Appleton's longtime store to new premises along the city's central artery, Broadway. The new building, a Greek Revival–style structure with soaring exterior Ionic columns, was "one of the most prominent edifices of the city."[38] When Appleton moved in, he left the exterior largely untouched, with one significant exception. Onto the previously blank entablature, he affixed large marble-esque letters spelling APPLETON. More a brand than a sign, this addition manifests what historian David Henkin has termed the "monumental architecture of the written word" and names the building before the business.[39]

This monumental typology was continued in the interior of the store, extensively remodeled from its previous occupants, the Society Library. Described as "the largest room (without obstructions) in New York," the 60- by 100-foot bookstore's expansive, uninterrupted sight lines encouraged a dwarfing, rather than intimate, effect.[40] Gleaming waxed floors reflected a brightly painted ceiling decorated with frescoed medallions. More ornate than the Ionic columns of the exterior, a double row of Corinthian columns shape the interior; classical Roman arches and alcoves with decorative busts survey the aisles, and 270 feet of shining oak shelving display books in

---

[37] Raven, *Bookscape*, 58. [38] "Appleton's New Head-quarters," 83.

[39] Henkin, *City Reading*, 50.

[40] "Messrs. Appleton's New Bookstore," *New York Observer and Chronicle*, January 19, 1854: 22. *American Periodical Series*.

Figure 2 Prevost, "D. Appleton & Co., formerly N.Y. Library Building, Broadway between Leonard Street & Catharine Lane [200 Broadway]" (1853–1857). Collections of the New York Historical Society.

a variety of colored, leather, and ornamental bindings. Contemporary descriptions celebrated the showroom's elegance and artistic effect. The architecture and design of this space attracted conspicuous attention to itself rather than to the books it housed.

The spatial design of the new Broadway store was a significant departure from the previous store, which was more aligned with the bookshop as intimate domestic space. Three times narrower and half the length of the

Figure 3 "Interior View of Appleton's Book Store, 346 & 348 Broadway, New York" (1856). The New York Public Library.

new store, the previous Appleton's was cozy.[41] An engraving of the interior included in an 1847 catalogue shows books crowding walls, shelves, and tables and patrons browsing and relaxing amid embroidered lace table-cloths. In this earlier store the wares – the books – were the primary attraction. The move to the new building promised Appleton not only a larger space for his growing bookselling firm, but also an opportunity to remodel – to reinvent – the form of bookstore. The new monumental bookstore was an aesthetic experience, less about books than a constructed environment and collective experience. If the corners of cozy bookstores

[41] Qtd in Wolfe, *The House of Appleton*, 58, from an unnamed contemporary periodical in the NYHS collections.

suggest immobility and solitude, the soaring open space and grand scales of the monumental bookstore engender sociality and mobility, both physical and social.

Part of a broader nineteenth-century pattern in enlarging stores, Appletons and other retailers drew on increasingly ornate architectural and design elements previously reserved for civic spaces such as Federal Hall and the Merchant's Exchange.[42] Linked with the midcentury rise of the first department stores – A. T. Stewart opened his "marble palace" just a few years before and a few blocks south of Appleton's – commercial institutions went grander. These bookstores were lauded for their extravagant size and design. Lackington, Allen, & Company's Finsbury Square, London store was perhaps the first and one of the best known of these monumental stores. Grand and classically allusive even in name, his "Temple of the Muses," established in 1794, featured huge windows, floor to ceiling bookshelves with climbing ladders, multiple floors of books and lounging rooms, and a central desk built into a multilevel columned atrium.[43] The ubiquity of illustrations and engravings of Lackington's interior reprinted in newspapers, periodicals, and contemporary guides to London emphasize the store as spectacle in itself.

Even outside the publishing and bookselling centers of London and New York, booksellers drew on monumental forms. William Young's newly built 1864 bookstore in Troy, New York, was fronted with cast-iron Corinthian columns, and at four stories, dwarfed the surrounding buildings. Inside, a paper warehouse and offices occupied the upper floors, while the "spacious" ground-floor bookstore featured "long rows of shelves filled with books."[44] Other booksellers drew on monumental and classical

[42] Raven, *Bookscape*, 150.

[43] A number of illustrations depicting the interior of Lackington's shop were produced. See, for instance, William Wallis (fl.1816–1855) after Thomas Hosmer Shepherd (1793–1864), *Temple of the Muses, Finsbury Square*. London: Jones, 1828. Princeton University Library, www.princeton.edu/~graphicarts/temple%20of%20the%20muses.html.

[44] Waite, *The Architecture of Downtown Troy*, 89.

Figure 4 "Messrs. Lackington, Allen & Co., Temple of the Muses, Finsbury Square" (1828). Courtesy of Princeton University Library.

iconography in their store's advertising materials. William Colman featured Corinthian columns and carved stones in his booksellers' label.[45]

Tied to a social geography of economic aspiration and social mobility, the monumental bookstore marks consumerism as an act of civic participation. Architectural historian Dell Upton notes that these grand classical and revival elements in commercial buildings evoke a geography of refinement that "flatter[s] the lofty and aspiring."[46] To buy books in this space was to assert one's own taste and membership in a fashionable community. Here, the bookstore typology does not suggest an individualized experience, reflective practice, or escape, but, rather, a normative social community based in a shared spatial and aesthetic

[45] William Colman, bookseller label. Collections of the American Antiquarian Society.

[46] Upton, *Another City*, 155.

experience. Books are the set pieces meant to be appreciated as objects within a larger stage. If spaces for reading are offered, openness and visibility mark reading as a public performance.

Monumental typologies remain the unifying element and predominant feature of many "famous" bookstores today. Rizzoli's former store in New York City featured cast iron chandeliers, ornately decorated ceiling vaulting, and a grand Diocletian window.[47] The Foyles remodel that concerned customers feared might eliminate the nooks and crannies they loved introduced "towering" windows and a large central atrium. In the new monumental design, a single wide staircase, echoing those of grand theaters, connects the eight alternating levels of verticality.[48] In the Netherlands, the well-known Selexyz Dominicanen Bookstore fits a black steel multilevel store in the shell of a former Dominican church. "The sheer, monumental and asymmetrical frame" of the bookstore is a three-story "filigreed confessional of books."[49] Indeed, the discourse of sacred monumentality is tied to this typology; New York's The Strand is "that cathedral of second-hand books," another bookstore is a "shrine."[50] Discussed as "The World's Most Beautiful Bookstore" by National Geographic in 2019, Buenos Aires' Ateneo Grand Splendid, a "temple of books," incorporates the palatial dimensions, rounded balconies, and ornate frescoes of the early-twentieth-century former theater.[51]

The Ateneo Grand Splendid and the Selexyz Dominicanen bookstores, like Appletons and others before them, also derive physical and symbolic monumentality from the former functions of their buildings. The Grand Splendid was once a theater; the Selexyz Dominicanen a cathedral. Appleton's new monumental store took over the former home of the Society Library. When describing the relationship between the new flagship Foyles bookstore and the former arts college that occupied the space, the architect, Alex Lifschutz, explicitly connects the two spaces in an associative

[47] von la Valette, *Cool Shops*, 118–121. [48] Campbell, "Foyles' New Flagship."

[49] Klanten and Feireiss, *Build-On*, 154.

[50] Qtd in Carrión, *Bookshops*, 132; Edwards, "On the Experience."

[51] Howard, "This is the world's."

geography: "This project inserts the most famous and much-loved book-shop into the inspirational former home of one of the UK's most creative arts schools."[52] Theaters, libraries, colleges, churches, and then bookstores. The civic and sacred associations embedded in these physical spaces form a sort of temporal socio-spatial continuum whereby the bookstore acquires cultural significance. All but divorced from its commercial function of selling books (if it hopes to stick around), the bookstore is instead natur-alized as a cultural institution.

Images of these remarkable monumental stores circulate on social media and reappear again and again in bookstore tourism articles that feature and rank bookstores across the world. This genre creates a type of feedback loop whereby social value and recognition is expanded, elevating these bookstores in the cultural imagination while they are simultaneously abstracted from context and commercial function. Here, monumentality is linked to mobility, aspiration, status, and a shared communal experience through digital virality and tourism. While these bookstores are locally emplaced, they are insistently global, available to viewers anywhere to admire and perhaps aspire to visit. In addition to those bookstores men-tioned above, other commonly mentioned stores include the 17,000-square-foot Taipei bookstore, Eslite Dunnan, the Livraria Lello in Porto, Portugal, with its sweeping staircase and neo-Gothic architecture, and Mexico City's soaring Cafebreria El Pendulo.[53] Indeed, the ubiquitous superlative lists of "Best Bookstores" form another discursive layer of monumentality. The most, the best, the biggest. The superlative monumentalizes. In these lists and posts, the store itself – or rather, its carefully photographed interior – is the commodity being circulated. These stores are famous not for the goods

---

[52] Campbell, "Foyles New Flagship."

[53] See, for instance, Frances Cha, "Bookmark this! World's Best Bookstores," *CNN Travel*, August 4, 2015, https://edition.cnn.com/travel/article/worlds-coolest-bookstores-new/index.html; Ania James, "15 Best Bookshops Around the World," (blog), April 12, 2019, https://the-travelling-twins.com/best-bookshops-around-the-world/; Ashley Lutz, "18 Bookstores Every Book Lover Must Visit At Least Once," *Insider*, February 5, 2014, www.businessinsider.com/best-bookstores-in-the-world-2014-2014-2.

they sell, but rather for their built environments and broad recognition. The interplay of built space, representations of that space, and social exchange create the monumental bookstore.

Of course, the two material and symbolic typologies discussed here – the monumental and the intimate – are neither mutually exclusive nor deterministic. Individuals choose what to attend to and respond in myriad ways to spatial messages. And aspects of both typologies can certainly be layered within the same material spaces and imaginative geographies of book buyers. The Last Bookstore in Los Angeles, for instance, engages both registers. Previously a bank (the ultimate civic-commercial institution), the Romanesque Spring Arts Tower, built in 1914, features huge ground-level double-story windows framed in brass, extended cornices with decorative friezes, and an arched marble entry with fluted pilasters and carved entablature. The monumentality continues inside, where the 10,000-square-foot open atrium is supported by rows of marble Doric columns. Books as well take on architectural forms, shaped into archways, walls, and windows in elaborate book art installations. Yet the owner of the Last Bookstore, Josh Spencer, explicitly describes his bookstore within the framework of a domestic space. It is a "huge living room," he says, "a home away from home."[54] Overstuffed chairs, alcoves in the mezzanine levels, and the book arts displays divide space, creating those spatial corners that facilitate privacy and introspection.

The layered spatial and discursive registers in this space point to the complexity and contingency of experiences of space. These two spatial typologies, however, make clear that the bookstore is never just selling books. The intimate and the monumental concretize differing values associated with books, as extensions of the private self or as cultural and aesthetic commodities.

2.2 Stacks and Stock

When the child protagonist of Susan Warner's 1850 bestselling novel, *The Wide, Wide World*, enters a bookshop, she encounters a sensory wonderland. Young Ellen Montgomery is thrilled by the scene:

[54] Howitt, *Welcome to The Last Bookstore*.

Children's books, lying in tempting confusion near the door,
immediately fastened Ellen's eyes and attention. She opened
one, and was already deep in the interest of it, when the
word "Bibles" struck her ear. Mrs. Montgomery was desir-
ing the shopman to show her various kinds and sizes that she
might choose from among them. Down went Ellen's book,
and she flew to the place where a dozen different Bibles were
presently displayed. Ellen's wits were ready to forsake her.
Such beautiful Bibles she had never seen; she pored in
ecstasy over their varieties of type and binding, and was
very evidently in love with them all.[55]

In this description, we follow the burgeoning-book buyer Ellen from
display to display. The pile of children's books, "lying in tempting confusion," first seduces her. Their location by the door attests to the potent draw
and sales potential of these cheaper juvenile books, while their haphazard
arrangement invites tactile engagement – pick through them, open them,
read them. Then, an overheard conversation with a bookstore clerk draws
Ellen's attention to the Bibles. Speaking to a different consumer logic, the
Bible display suggests a more rational organization by size and binding.

This brief scene underscores the significance of the interior spatial
organization of the bookstore and its books. Shelves, tables, and displays
form the topographies of bookstores, carving and organizing space, creating
physical ranges, canyons, and valleys traversed by customers. Likewise, the
planned organization of stock, its placements and adjacencies, and its displays create an epistemological map charting intellectual pathways and
connections. In short, the interior layout of the bookstore guides both the
feet and minds of book buyers.

The humble bookshelf and the book table, made invisible beneath the
stock they support, provide the material conditions for these associations
and experiences. And their forms come in all varieties: built-in wall bookshelves, freestanding shelving, movable shelves. In his deep history of the
bookshelf, from ancient chests to book presses to the more modern book

---

[55] Warner, *The Wide, Wide World*, 34.

stacks, Henry Petrowki emphasizes bookshelves as technological systems. Experimentations in display and shelving is a common feature of bookstores. Profiling "ingenious" bookseller F. A. Munger in Newburgh, NY, in 1918, a two-page *Publisher's Weekly* spread celebrated his shelving invention for its ability to display over 1,000 titles.[56] The "new book rack," which consisted of a custom-built table with shelving below and a tabletop display of three risers extending upward, featured books in all configurations – horizontally arranged in the lower shelves, lying flat or with spine upward on the tabletop and slotted upright facing outward on the risers. Credited with powering his book sales, "Munger Book Racks" were later advertised and sold by New York City booksellers Baker & Taylor Co. in their manual, *Bookselling*.[57]

More recently, a new 2019 Barnes & Noble "concept store" in Columbia, MD, introduced redesigned bookshelves and tables. In this smaller, more intimate store, two "book theaters" at the center front and back featured a round, multitiered table atop a larger round carpeted area. The theaters, visually distinguished from the surrounding wood flooring, spotlighted new and specially curated books. Aisles of shelves with transparent dividers instead of customary vertical wood dividers, visually created a continuous shelf and guided the browser's eye along an uninterrupted horizontal line.[58] Another fascinating shelving innovation in Beijing's Mumokuteki Concept Bookstore, housed in the former basement equipment room of a large mall, hinges on translucent rotating walls that use round wooden dowels to anchor adjustable metal shelves.[59] These shelving walls can be configured to create an open room or rotated to create divided segments of the store.

All of these shelves, displays, theaters, and tables act on our processes of moving through and engaging in the space of the bookstore. We roam the perimeter of the store before targeting a row or we zigzag through book stacks or browse accessible displays. We tilt our heads to the side to read spine titles on books shelved vertically; we crouch or sit in place to examine books below our sight line. We pick up books stacked on tables. Our reading of the shelves may follow the reading of pages in books; in English,

[56] "Successful Bookselling," 12–13. [57] *Bookselling*.
[58] Kwisnek, "Get an In-Depth Look." [59] Morris, "LUO Studio."

top to bottom and right to left. Or perhaps a display or pile of books invites a more haphazard scanning. As Roger Chartier asserts, "reading is always a practice embodied in acts, spaces, and habits."[60] Even as they disappear beneath the books they hold, bookshelves and tables frame, facilitate, and direct this embodied practice within the bookstore.

The arrangement of a bookstore – its shelving, displays, sales counter, seating areas – are dictated by any number of factors, including practical and economic exigencies. For instance, in large corporate bookseller chains, appearances and displays, in addition to stock, are often dictated and standardized.[61] Regardless of the rationales driving design, store layout influences movement, forms of engagement, and purchasing behavior in complex ways. To this end, business experts, consumer psychologists, and marketing professionals analyze the work of store layout on buying practices. Manuals for aspiring booksellers describe best practices in terms of store layout and navigability; the space of the store is divided and subdivided to maximize engagement and profit potential. In its course on Bookshop Marketing, for example, The South African Booksellers Association notes that individuals need a "landing strip" upon entering a bookstore in which they reorient themselves as customers in the store.[62] Termed a "decompression zone" by consumer researcher Paco Underhill, this threshold might be marked by a change in lighting or flooring.[63] Stock placed there is often overlooked by the customer, but deeply discounted stock might pause the shopper and facilitate that transition.

Yet consumer behavior can be fickle. Underhill narrates an example of a bookstore that placed a table of discounted books beside the entrance which attracted attention and increased sales, but decreased traffic to other areas of the store: "Shoppers would enter, hit the bargain table, then maybe visit one or two more displays, but they never strayed far from the front of the store before heading to the cashier."[64] Other studies seek to understand this consumer behavior. In their multidimensional study of customer experiences in bookshops, economist Michela Addis found that individuals

---

[60] Chartier, *The Order of Books*, 3.   [61] Loesch, "Why Working."

[62] SA Booksellers Association, *Bookshop Marketing*.

[63] Underhill, *Why We Buy*, 43–45.   [64] Underhill, *Why We Buy*, 22–23.

patronizing "chain" bookshops, who tend to rely less on bookseller inter-action, preferred a controlled and standardized experience in which elements like signs, colors, and visual merchandizing were easily deciphered.[65] In addition, and supporting research by business experts, an architectural study of a grid layout in a bookstore highlighted the importance of visual exposure, including clear sight lines and end displays, along major paths to increase product engagement.[66] What the eye sees, the hands engage with.

These analyses work to rationalize human behavior in relation to space and the built environment, and ultimately, in the context of business and consumer research, to optimize and control movement and experience. The paradox of the "impulse aisle" is that it is a managed and disciplined space.[67] But as spatial theorist Michel de Certeau has written, disciplined space is regularly undermined and resisted through "everyday practices" and the "lived space" of individuals.[68] De Certeau's suggestive theorization of the act of walking argues that walking is an individual and social practice through which the individual modifies the material structures and meanings of space. As a spatial practice, walking creates space. The wandering trajectories and passing by of walking reconfigure planned and disciplined space and thereby reshape the social functions of space. Echoed succinctly by Gaston Bachelard, "Inhabited space transcends geometrical space."[69] In the context of the bookstore and store layouts, the empiricization of spatial experience is regularly undercut by individuals who, in wandering, pausing, sitting, and engaging, remodel the material and social space of the bookstore.

If the wandering among bookshelves and aisles and other physical spaces creates the lived experience of the bookstore, the organization of its stock offers an itinerary. This is an intellectual journey, one in which genre classifications and adjacencies suggest relationships between forms of knowledge and shape reading practices. The placement and organization

---

[65] Addis, "Understanding the Customer Journey," 31.

[66] Lu and Seo, "Developing Visibility Analysis."

[67] SA Booksellers Association, *Bookshop Marketing*.

[68] de Certeau, *The Practice of Everyday Life*, 96.

[69] Bachelard, *The Poetics of Space*, 47.

of books in a book shop varies historically and by individual establishment. Before the mid-nineteenth century, depending on the type of store, goods might be piled on counters, stuffed in chests, and, at times, mixed with the personal possessions of the proprietor.[70] When New Yorker George Templeton Strong entered a bookstore on a mid-June day in 1839, he "noticed a gigantic basket full" of old books, but after exploring this basket, pronounced them all "sad trash."[71] Later, interested in an edition of Robert Southey's poems, Strong wrote in his diary that he "hunted for a good while" among the bookstore's shelves.[72] The operative verbs "noticed" and "hunted"—calling to mind an accidental, wandering, and uncertain search – describe a space in flux and a stock organization not immediately intelligible to the customer or easily navigated. Of course, even if a bookstore's organizational logic was not easily or quickly deciphered by the customer, the bookseller would likely have a perfect knowledge of where and how his books were stocked. The "logic of discovery," then, is a matter of perspective as well as a possible deliberate sales technique.

Just a few doors south in Homer Franklin's establishment at 180 Broadway, Strong and other customers would have found a store stocked with a broad array of books – Bibles piled next to novels, poetry book-ending law books, and philosophy, reference, and travel books mixed among the shelves. The organizational conventions in today's bookstores – genre categories, alphabetization of topic, author, or title – were not modes practiced in Franklin's 1840 store. In literary historian Ronald Zboray's statistical analysis of three Franklin store inventories between 1839 and 1840, he calculates a high likelihood of finding technical books next to religious texts, suggesting specific antebellum structures of knowledge. Stocking the American Fruit Garden Companion (1838) next to Lectures on Homilectics and Preaching (1834), for example, pairs the books, Zboray argues, in a complementary project of self-help informed by Protestant ideology. Likewise, the period's concern with the effect of emerging scientific theories on religious doctrine is in turn evidenced by Charles Lyell's Principles of Geology (1830–1833) stacked next to English

---

[70] Upton, *Another City*, 150.
[71] Strong, *The Diary of George Templeton Strong*, 107. [72] Ibid., 46.

clergyman Samuel Bloomfield's philological study of The Greek Testament (1837).[73] Stock organization can thus be a reflection of epistemological constructions; more than a marketing strategy, the arrangement of stock is "a response to the prospective customer, a 'reading' of the reader."[74]

Twentieth- and twenty-first-century bookstores maintain diverse stock organizations, all of which likewise reveal insights into how the bookstore or how the bookstore's customers construct and value knowledge. In the 1950s, Foyles of London organized its stock by publisher, as did the long-running Book Exchange in Durham, North Carolina.[75] This organizational logic privileges the publisher, as opposed to the author, as the arbiter and authority of knowledge. It also offers insight into the book as an evolving material form and the life and death of publishing houses. Longtime patron of the Book Exchange Kate Ariail notes,

> In this dying bookshop were preserved, for a little longer, the names and small remains of deceased publishers, and in some places the spines on the shelves charted the changes (or not) in book design over decades. You could see the evolution of the Penguins and the Pelicans, rank after rank, mutating in size, color, typeface; and the long consistency of Cambridge University Press.[76]

On material forms, the common practice of separating hardbacks and paperbacks suggests a qualitative distinction beyond simply price. And arranging books by color, as the upper level of Saraiva book shop in Rio de Janeiro does, adds an additional aesthetic dimension to the cultural work of book stock organization.[77]

While subject headings tend to be the most common modern-day organizational pattern, subject categories are neither fixed nor universal. Travel bookshops are often organized geographically. The Altaïr book shop in Barcelona clusters traditional travel guides and maps with poetry,

---

[73] Zboray, *A Fictive People*, 147–148. [74] Ibid., 137.

[75] Carrión, *Bookshops*, 30; Petroski, *The Book on the Bookshelf*, 240–241.

[76] Ariail, "Durham's Book Exchange." [77] Griffiths, "Colour-coded Books."

fiction, and essays by country and continent.[78] This organization suggests
that in order to truly navigate a new place, one needs literature as much as
a map. The American author Verlyn Klinkenborg says of stock arrangement in John Sandoe Books in London, "its windows and staircases [are]
crammed with books, one genre fading into the next, the occasional sense
that the shelving here has been done by free association . . . the books at
John Sandoe seem to belong to an extensive cousinage, a kinship of ink."
For Klinkenborg, this "kinship of ink" "made me feel discerning and
capacious as a reader."[79] This comment explicitly highlights how the spatial
logic of stock placement shapes conceptions of ourselves as readers and
thinkers.

Subject headings, and more generally shelving and organization, as an
explicit epistemological exercise is a necessary political activity for bookstores engaged with social movements. In San Francisco's famous City
Lights Bookstore, owner Nancy Peters explains the store's approach to
knowledge subjects:

> Media criticism is shelved under "Commodity Aesthetics."
> We put mystery and criminology under "Evidence." We
> don't just have "politics," we have "Green Politics."
> There's a section on "topographies," but it's not just geo-
> graphy. It covers the topography of the body, too.[80]

Categories like "Class War" and "Stolen Continents" challenge and
subvert staid genre categories and articulate alternative modes for understanding information and the world around us. In her examination of
American feminist bookstores, Kristen Hogan has proposed the term
"feminist shelf" as a means of defining how feminist booksellers have
utilized spatial organization and adjacency, along with store programming,
to help customers develop new critical vocabularies and connective threads
between different subjects and titles, to shape reading practices, and to

---

[78] Carrión, *Bookshops*, 28.   [79] "About."
[80] Emblidge, "City Lights Bookstore," 34.

encourage a feminist ethics of dialogue.[81] A single title might be found in a variety of sections, speaking to different relationalities and reading practices. In one example Hogan mentions, former Canadian poet laureate Dionne Brand's poetry collection *No Language Is Neutral* (1990) might be found in a Poetry section, but could also be shelved in sections such as Caribbean Women, Lesbian Non-Fiction, or Black Canadian Women, with different books beside it available for browsing and forming new conceptual maps.[82]

Bookshelves also create material sites for shared solidarity and awareness. In a 1988 issue of the *Feminist Bookstore News*, Joni Seager of New Words Bookstore in Cambridge, Massachusetts, described how the store created an international women's fiction section, "almost an entire wall," in recognition of the United Nations' Decade of Women (1975–1985). Creating this section not only increased sales of these titles, Seager writes, but in making them accessible and visible, put "consciousness on the shelf."[83] For Paul Coates, the father of writer and scholar Ta-Nehisi Coates, his Baltimore store The Black Book in the 1970s was never a business. Rather, he says, "we were engaged in a political movement. And the books . . . were bullets that we fired at the enemy and we fired at the brains of people who needed information to liberate themselves."[84] Drawing on a metaphor of war, his was a battle for knowledge and political rights. In Britain, historian Lucy Delap emphasizes how the radical bookstores from the 1960s onward "provided distinctive material sites" that served "to focus radical political commitments."[85]

In addition to the edifying and epistemological work of subject headings and stock organization, bookshelves can also make visible and revalue diverse identities. When Beverly Haynes enters Black-owned Los Angeles bookstore Eso Won, she explains that seeing books "for me and by people like me [. . .] grounds me and molds me as a black woman."[86]

---

[81] Hogan, *The Feminist Bookstore Movement*, 109. [82] Ibid., 135.

[83] Seager, "International Women," 42.

[84] Qtd in Davis, *From Head Shops to Whole Foods*, 60.

[85] Delap, "Feminist Bookshops," 172.

[86] Jennings, "Eso Won Books," para. 10. Qtd in Kinder, *The Radical Bookstore*, 169.

Amid white landscapes of exclusion, Black-owned bookstores carve space for Black subjectivities. Further explaining the significance of the link between representation on shelves and identity, Greg Newton of the LGBTQ-focused Bureau of General Services in New York stresses that for the queer community, "'bookstores were where we learned about ourselves.' Pointing to the shelves, Newton said with pride, 'It belongs to us. This is our heritage.'"[87] By claiming space on a bookstore's shelves, books focused on the voices and experiences of marginalized identities claim space for these individuals in communities and in larger society.

When categories of identity and books intersect, which book covers are faced outward on the shelf or featured in a table or end display not only concretize representation, but can also can also signal implicit value judgments. In Toi Derricotte's poem "Bookstore" (2019), the speaker enters a shop seeking children's books "written by or for black folks."[88] When the speaker asks the white clerk for help,

> She looks as if she doesn't understand. Maybe she has never
> heard the words black folk before. Maybe she thinks
> I'm white and mean it as a put-down. Since I'm white-
> looking, I better make it clear. "It's for my brother's son.
> 'black folks,' black people . . . you know . . . like me!"
> As quickly as she can, she pulls books from the lower
> shelves and loads my arms until the books are falling on the floor.

Though the clerk seeks to assuage any doubt of the depth of representation of books by and about Black people, the poem ends with the declaration, "the names of the missing are clear." Even more than the "missing names" and despite the "loads" of books presented, it's their location on the "lower/shelves" that speaks volumes. With the line break emphasizing "lower," we are meant to understand how shelving placement communicates value.

Ultimately, visual prominence is a persuasive tool. Whether the goal of persuasion is to convert to a cause, to reinforce a sense of identity, to create

[87] Qtd in Kinder, *The Radical Bookstore*, 170. [88] Derricotte, "Bookstore," 188.

an inclusive space, to buy a book, or to do a little of each, the spatial aspects of book stocking – from physical shelves to organizational logics – function in dense social, material, and intellectual networks.

2.3 Reflection

This section has sought to illustrate the ways in which the space of the bookstore shapes ideas and practices of reading, identity, knowledge, and community. While the emphasis of this discussion has been on specific typologies of the built environment and spatial logics of book organization, there are additional spatial considerations that merit closer attention, including the rise of cafes in bookstores and their historical links to café culture or the use of dedicated or improvised event space in bookstores. In addition, children's book sections in bookstores offer rich grounds for analysis of design, color, and placement, and I would argue the bookstore bulletin board or noticeboard deserves its own dedicated study as a space for community-building. Considered together, all of these spatial aspects inform, enrich, and complicate the cultural, commercial, and social dimensions of bookstores.

3 Streets: Books, Boundaries, and Belonging

When twentieth-century bookseller Kathryn Magnolia Johnson explained why she traveled the nation selling books about Black life and history, she insisted the books be brought physically to readers:

> I knew the books that would help the Negro to understand his honorable place in America. The question was how to get him to buy them. You can't buy books from pictures, as you can dresses and farm implements. They won't show up in a mail order catalogue. I knew the man or woman must handle the book, see what was in it, before he would put money down for it. So I bought my Ford and became an itinerant bookseller.[89]

From the urban book carts and perambulating book peddlers of the nineteenth century to the automobile booksellers and sidewalk book vendors of the twentieth and twenty-first centuries, the street has always provided both a means and an active site for putting books in hands. In addition to Johnson's "itinerant bookseller," diverse labels given booksellers on the road highlight the contours of the trade: book peddler, book hawker, subscription agent, colporteur, traveling bookseller, canvasser, newsboy, and sidewalk bookseller and vendor.[90] As an inclusive term for these different types of bookselling, I use "street bookselling" to describe forms of bookselling united by the reliance on the road and its sidewalk for a sales network or selling space.

In contrast to the bounded walls and defined economic purpose of the bookstore and shop, the street seems open, boundless, an informal space outlining and connecting formal spaces and structures. In literature and

---

[89] Ovington, "Selling Race Pride," 114.

[90] These English-language labels represent only a fraction of terms for street vendors; an array of local and regionally specific terms highlight the ubiquitous nature of street-based commerce. For instance, India has a rich vocabulary for street vending, including *pheriwalla*, *rehripatri walla*, and footpath *dukandars*. Graaff and Ha, *Street Vending*, 2.

media, the road often functions as an open, liberated space where the individual might escape (or be alienated from) social and political forms. Jack Kerouac took to the American road to chart his own path away from 1950s societal conformity; Thelma and Louise grabbed the wheel of their own stories and escaped their lives in their 1966 powder blue Thunderbird convertible. Yet the freedom of the road is limited and selective, most notably on the bases of gender and race. Thelma and Louise's story ended not in life but in their deaths. For the Black characters of Misha Green's television adaptation of *Lovecraft Country*, free travel on the road is itself a fiction, blocked by segregation and exclusionary all-white sundown towns and navigable only with the alternative maps of Uncle George's *Safe Negro Travel Guide*, based on the real-life *Negro Motorist Green Book*. The transgressive potential of the road is unequally accessible and always subject to legal and social controls.

This tension between openness and control engages questions of mobility and access. Who can use certain roads and roadspaces and who cannot? What does the ability to move or to stay signify for different populations? How do different power structures – political, legal, social – shape street space? How do forms of surveillance seek to control roads and streets? Booksellers on the road must navigate these tensions. Experienced as an open space, the road offers booksellers a means to expand book markets, reimagine the self, and consolidate communities. But a variety of local conditions constrain access, including political and legal policies, licensing and copyright restrictions, physical geographies, and social mores.

These issues of access reveal competing and contested geographies of belonging and exclusion associated with the street. Belonging is a spatial construct, negotiated through material, discursive, and social means. The material landscape, for instance, can communicate what belongs and what doesn't; a planter installed where a sidewalk bookseller sets up or a police checkpoint on the road in the segregated American South mark boundaries and exclusion. Belonging is also a discursive mode "which constructs, claims, justifies, or resists forms" of inclusion and exclusion.[91] Itinerant bookseller memoirs, editorial defenses of sidewalk bookselling, and court

---

[91] Antonsich, "Searching for Belonging," 644.

arguments against summonses make discursive space for belonging. Lastly, as geographers Kathleen Mee and Sarah Wright note, "belonging is central to understanding the social control of space."[92] Following Lefebvre, since spatial organization is a cultural product of power, belonging is mediated through social categories of class, race, and gender, among others.[93] Yet in his extension of Lefebvre's theories, Edward Soja highlights ways in which "directly *lived*" space – what he terms Thirdspace – offers transformative possibilities: "these lived spaces of representation are thus the terrain for the generation of 'counterspaces.'"[94] Geographies of belonging, enmeshed in existing material, power, and authority structures, in other words, can be reimagined and reshaped through the lived experience of space.

This section examines the street and street bookselling as a dynamic space and practice for navigating, transgressing, and redrawing cultural, social, and legal boundaries of belonging for the bookseller and their communities of customer-readers. Bookselling, in particular, offers a valuable lens to understand the dynamics of belonging and exclusion due to the status of the book as both a commercial and a cultural artifact. Invoking the perceived social good of the book is a rhetorical and, at times, legal stance assumed both by street booksellers and by regulating organizations. Selling books on the road, whether from a cart, a car, or a sidewalk table, is often uplifted as a higher mission of circulating knowledge and information. This cultural value associated with the book separates the street bookseller from other vendors, exposing both the fluid nature of the book as commodity and the opportunities and limits of the street as a bookselling space. Street bookselling thus both elucidates and challenges the contested social and legal boundaries of road and street space and expands the complex spatial and cultural geography of bookselling beyond the walls of the bookstore.

Though street bookselling has a long global history, this section focuses on street bookselling in the United States from the eighteenth to the twenty-first centuries, since local contexts, culture, and geographies shape the trade.

---

[92] Mee and Wright, "Geographies of Belonging," 772.
[93] Lefebvre, *The Production of Space.* [94] Soja, *Thirdspace*, 67–68.

The first subsection focuses on traveling booksellers and examines under-studied itinerant bookseller memoirs of nineteenth- and twentieth-century women and Black booksellers. Then, the section turns to contemporary sidewalk bookselling in New York City.

3.1 The Itinerant Bookseller: Mobility and Geographies of Belonging

"Why not try a little peripatetic enterprise?" asked *Publisher's Weekly* in March of 1879.[95] Though calling for print salespeople, this question is a caption for American culture more broadly. From Huck Finn's closing promise to "light out for the territory" to the stories of pilgrims, pioneers, and migrants, stories of wandering wind through American history and culture. The road provides a path for physical and social mobility. Two organizing principles of American space and identity, the nineteenth-century's western expansionist Manifest Destiny and the American Dream of the twentieth century with its spatial locus in the expanding suburbs dependent on the automobile, link geographical mobility to social ascent. Yet the mobility promised by the road was also used as a weapon, a means not for freeing but for coercion and sequestering, as the Trail of Tears and the routes of the domestic slave trade attest.

The road and mobility, then, is never neutral, never just physical. As human geographer Tim Cresswell argues, motion is both embodied and socially produced.[96] Quoting David Delaney, Creswell continues, "human mobility implicates *both* physical bodies moving through material land-scapes *and* categorical figures moving through representational spaces."[97] The road, therefore, is both a physical place and a meaning-producing space, one through which social relationships and cultural meaning are navigated, negotiated, and produced.

For booksellers taking on "a little peripatetic enterprise," mobility was, of course, practical; they needed to sell books. A history of bookselling on American roads is long and varied, stretching from the early independent

---

[95] "Booksellers as Local Agents," *Publisher's Weekly* (March 8, 1879), 279. Qtd in Hackenberg, "The Subscription Publishing Network," 66.

[96] Cresswell, *On the Move*, 3. [97] Ibid., 4.

book peddler who would replenish his stock at country stores to more formal distribution relationships between publisher and traveling agent, earliest attempted – with debatable contemporary success but important future implications – by eighteenth-century Philadelphia publisher Mathew Carey and his loquacious agent Mason Locke "Parson" Weems. Following technological changes in printing, improved transportation networks, and expansion of the book trades, nineteenth-century general and specialized subscription publishers directed travelling agents to assigned regions to canvass for subscriptions.[98] Carrying prospectus copies of subscription titles, these agents joined colporteurs, who had long played a central role in distributing religious tracts and texts throughout the nation.[99] Door-to-door book agents continued the peripatetic book trade in the twentieth century as the material challenges of "bringing the book and the reader together" continued.[100]

And while street bookselling was one practical way of making this connection between book and reader, travelling booksellers also invest their bookselling with diverse ideological, social, and individual meanings. Scholars of early America and the nineteenth century have recognized the ways in which itinerant bookselling provided a means for circulating new ideas in an expanding and expansive country. Books, as well as periodicals and newspapers, have always been "ambassadors of thought."[101] Culture, Creswell emphasizes, is more about "routes than roots."[102] These routes, the roads and rails and rivers on which booksellers traversed, link physical and ideological circulation in a broader project of shaping cultural values. Prominent puritan Cotton Mather knew this when he wrote in his diary of "an old *Hawker*," on a March day in 1683, "who will fill this Countrey with devout and useful Books, if I will direct him."[103] Two hundred years later, publisher William Garretson & Co. echoed the moral role of itinerant booksellers in their assertion that "An agent with good books is a moral benefactor. He goes into the highways, byways, and dark places of the land,

---

[98] Hackenberg, "The Subscription Publishing Network."

[99] Nord, *Faith in Reading*. [100] Qtd in West, *American Authors*, 45.

[101] Raven and Howsam, *Books between Europe and the Americas*, 1.

[102] Cresswell, *On the Move*, 1. [103] Mather, "11 d. 4m," 65.

and circulates knowledge where otherwise it would not penetrate."[104] This extended metaphor of itinerant booksellers carrying the light of knowledge and ideas to illuminate the uninformed darkness is commonly invoked in itinerant booksellers' own descriptions of their roles. The famous Mason Locke "Parson" Weems wrote in an 1810 letter to his publisher Mathew Carey, "the Country is in Darkness. Men's minds are uninform'd, their hearts bitter, and their manners savage. Humanity and Patriotism both cry aloud, Books Books, Books."[105] As both "true Philanthropist and prudent speculator," Weems paved the itinerant booksellers' commercial routes with moral purpose.[106]

In addition to the circulation of ideas, the mobility of the road gave travelling booksellers paths for social reinvention, both for their customers and themselves. Historian David Jaffee describes itinerancy in the early republic as "a stage in the life cycle as well as a method of social mobility in the fluid social world of the early republic."[107] While peddlers in general, with their clocks, portraits, and chairs, "promot[ed] the message of social transformation through the purchase of goods," the peddler also constructed "new self-identities" through physical and social mobility.[108] Farm sons might reinvent themselves in emerging commercial towns. For nineteenth-century philosopher Ralph Waldo Emerson, the "sturdy lad" who peddles will "walk abreast with his days" and "does not postpone his life, but lives already."[109] He engages in the act of self-creation. In the case of Sarah Emma Edmonds, a New Brunswick farm girl who set off to canvas Bibles in 1858, the road provided her an actual new life. Recreating herself as Frank Thompson, Edmonds enlisted in a Michigan regiment in the Civil War and later published a fictional account of her experience.[110] As Matt

---

[104] Qtd in Stern, "Dissemination of Popular Books," 80.

[105] Qtd in Zboray, *A Fictive People*, 39, Weems to Carey, July 30, 1810 in Emily Ellsworth Skeel (ed.), *Mason Locke Weems: His Work and His Ways*, 3 vols. (New York: private printing, 1929).

[106] Ibid. Weems to Carey, October 15, 1796.

[107] Jaffee, "Peddlers of Progress," 521.   [108] Ibid., 512–513.

[109] Emerson, "Self-Reliance," 275.

[110] Hackenberg, "The Subscription Publishing Network," 51.

Boehm notes of the relationship between peddling and literary production, "peddling's cultural appeal relied on the mythic aura of transformative potential."[111] Edmonds mobilized this transformative potential, using street bookselling to renegotiate the relations of belonging and transform herself and her future.

Entwined in the production of both culture and the self, the road provided, for booksellers especially, a path to assume cultural authority as an author as well. Edmonds' Civil War memoir offers one example; Parson Weems' prolific authorship of biographies and moralistic literature another.[112] Supported by access to diverse printed materials and reading communities and tastes gained through their physical mobility, itinerant bookseller-authors sauntered onto their own title pages. Drawing on Michel de Certeau's theorizations of the way that physical journeys map onto narrative structures, ambulating booksellers who write their own memoirs subvert and reshape prescribed or planned space through the performative and self-composing act of walking and writing.[113] Through their literary memoirs, in other words, travelling booksellers write themselves into belonging, remapping the social meanings of the road and the boundaries of identity.

For Annie Nelles Dumond, an itinerant bookseller in the 1860s Midwest, the social and spatial constrictions of gender catalyzed her itinerant book-selling career. Her memoir, *Annie Nelles, or The Life of a Book Agent* (1868), combines a likely sensationalized life story with a more verifiable recount-ing of her life as a travelling subscription bookseller.[114] In Nelles' telling,

---

[111]   Boehm, "Peddler Poets," 2.

[112]   On Weems as author, see Boehm, "Peddler Poets," and Garcia, "The 'curiou-saffaire' of Mason Locke Weems."

[113]   de Certeau, *The Practice of Everyday Life*, especially Ch. 7.

[114]   James L. Murphy tracks the inconsistencies and problems with substantiating evidence that suggest that aspects of Nelles' personal life as described in the memoir are either exaggerated or fabricated. Of her bookselling career, how-ever, he notes, "Beginning with Annie's attempts to earn a living as a book canvasser, however, greater verisimilitude takes hold" and he can "affirm that much of that aspect of her autobiography is probably true." See Murphy, "The 'Unbelievable' Odyssey," 180.

she turned to travelling bookselling to escape society's limitations on women following the breakdown of her second marriage. Largely confined to her home without a job, much like the caged birds she loves as pets, and without the reputational support of her husband, Nelles is forced into a gendered spatial and social immobility. This enforced stasis is, as geographer Doreen Massey emphasizes, a "crucial means of subordination."[115] Seeking to escape her socio-spatial confinement, Nelles replies to an advertisement for subscription sales agents in the *Chicago Tribune* and is contracted by publisher W. J. Holland to sell a Civil War historical fiction novel, *Tried and True, or Love and Loyalty: A Story of the Great Rebellion* (1866), in northern Illinois and Indiana.[116] Taking to the road as a canvasser offers Nelles a means of physical mobility as well as the possibility of transgressing social boundaries and remaking herself. The agent claims agency. Considering the balance of truth and exaggeration or fiction in her memoir, it's notable that Nelles' verifiable life as bookseller – not introduced until two-thirds into her memoir – gives her the identity she uses to title her book: *The Life of a Book Agent*.

Once on the road, Nelles challenges patriarchal social and spatial norms and works to recreate herself outside of normative conventions. Yet the road isn't an instant liberatory space for her. Like other single women navigating public space, Nelles must present herself as a widow because she "dreaded the loss of position" she feared might follow if potential customers knew she was estranged or divorced.[117] And while she can move freely by rail or by foot, she finds that rural roads are largely masculine spaces. In one notable and detailed scene, emphasized by an accompanying illustration in the memoir, she sits for several hours under a tree on the side of the road outside Elmwood, IL, awaiting a passing vehicle to travel to smaller adjacent towns. As a woman, she is again rendered immobile – relegated to the margins of the road as a passive bystander. Yet after awhile, a local farmer with a cart of shelled corn approaches and offers her a ride. Once Nelles climbs into his cart, he grows curious about her basket. Surprised to learn that the basket is filled with books and not foodstuffs and following

[115] Massey, *Space, Place, and Gender*, 179. [116] Dumond, *Annie Nelles*, 242.
[117] Ibid., 289.

some savvy wit and encouragement from Nelles, he picks up a volume and starts reading. Nelles continues,

> He laid down his whip, took the book, and handed the lines to me. He was soon absorbed in the book, and I drove on, while he took no note of anything at all. I could have driven the team to Chicago, and he would never have known the difference, so interested was he in the story he held in his hand.[118]

Reader, he bought the book. But more than a sale, this anecdote suggests a shift in power facilitated both by the road and the book. That the male farmer is enthralled by the book is an ironic and gendered inversion of the eighteenth-century alarmist critiques of women readers so absorbed in their novels that they neglect their domestic duties. And while her book commands the attention and actions of the farmer, Nelles takes control. Literally taking the reins, she commandeers the cart as her own, claiming both the physical road and its imagined potential for mobility – her "I could have driven the team to Chicago"—for herself. Here Nelles unsettles the concept of the road as a masculine space.[119] While she started immobile on its margins, Nelles uses bookselling as the means to reclaim the road as a freeing and empowering space.

Yet throughout her memoir – almost-hijacked cart aside – it is Nelles' *walking* that most reshapes the normative spatialities of the road. Her descriptions of bookselling are organized by her walking paths. "I finally reached Lawn Ridge," she writes of one canvassing excursion, "about four o'clock in the afternoon; having sold all the books with which I started. My long walk had made me very weary and footsore, but still I had done very well, and felt content."[120] Unlike the book that earlier gave Nelles agency and control on a masculinized road, here books and bookselling receive

---

[118] Ibid., 284, 287–288.

[119] In this challenge, Nelles anticipates twentieth-century women writers' critiques and transformations of gendered road space. See Ganser, *Roads of Her Own*.

[120] Dumond, *Annie Nelles*, 296.

WAITING FOR THE WAGON.

Figure 5 "Waiting for the Wagon," in Dumond, *Annie Nelles*, 284. Digital image through HathiTrust and Google, Inc.

only a past-tense and passive nod and the customers are elided completely; rather, it's the act of walking that accrues meaning on a narrative and emotional level. She feels content because she sold books, of course, but the sentence structure pairs the feeling of satisfaction and contentment with the "long walk," as if it's the walk itself that is the focal point.

A few days later, having exhausted the sales possibilities in her area, she resolves to direct her steps to Chillicothe, IL, the following day. "It was a bright, pleasant day," she remembers,

> and there being no conveyance at hand, and learning that the roads were good all the way, I set out, in the early morning, to walk there. It was quite an undertaking for me, considering that it was not my intention to stop by the way; but it must be remembered, that I had been practicing pedestrianism considerably of late, and I boldly essayed the march.[121]

Playing with the multiple denotations of "essay," the final line links the attempt of walking to the practice of writing – footsteps as penstrokes. In Nelles' claim to be "practicing pedestrianism," we read an early formulation of Michel de Certeau's spatial theory of walking. For de Certeau, the walker, especially in cities, engages in "pedestrian speech acts" that write the city, creating new geographies of connection and association that work to subvert or supersede planned and normative space.[122] The walker, in other words, rewrites the city by creating meaningful space and new social relationships outside the boundaries imposed by official structures and maps. In her hundreds of miles of pedestrianism, in her every footprint and then in the textual representation of these steps in her memoir, Nelles engages in these pedestrian speech acts, rewriting the road and herself. Ultimately, she challenges patriarchal societal structures of marriage and poverty that depend on women's immobility and reconstructs the road as a life-giving space for women booksellers.

From Nelles, we now turn to another bookseller who deployed the road to create a trajectory of resistance to social power relations. From 1922 to 1932, African-American bookseller Kathryn Magnolia Johnson sold her "Two Foot Shelf" of books by and about Black Americans from the back

---

[121] Ibid., 318. [122] de Certeau, *The Practice of Everyday Life*, 97–99.

seat of her Ford coupe. Johnson's explicit goal was to "help the Negro to understand his honorable place in America."[123] Unlike other itinerant booksellers, she was not tied to a specific publisher; rather, she selected her stock based on its potential to "sell race pride."[124] Driven by a mission to get books directly into people's hands, Johnson explains, "I bought my Ford and became an itinerant bookseller."[125]

Johnson's street bookselling was more than a practical means of selling books. Her car of books calls to mind Shannon Mattern's exploration of "fugitive libraries" that "respond to conditions of exclusion and oppression."[126] Fugitive libraries, independent and itinerant, resist being fixed and settled. Their fugitivity, Mattern argues, instead embodies, quoting from cultural theorist Fred Moten, "a spirit of escape and transgression of the proper and proposed."[127] Johnson's stock of books on Black American contributions were explicitly meant to resist their exclusion from dominant cultural and published narratives and to escape ongoing physical and social oppression. And as Jane Greenway Carr adds, Johnson's bookselling was an "activism that relied on mobility to be fully executed."[128] The transgressive potential of fugitivity is based in mobility. For Johnson, bookselling on the road offered a space for the physical and social mobility necessary to resist racist social structures and to build community through racial identity.

In her *Publishers Weekly* profile of Johnson, published in 1925, Mary White Ovington describes Johnson's bookselling accomplishments in both sales and spatial terms. In two and a half years, Johnson "has sold five thousand volumes of [books], has been in ten states and her speedometer registers twenty-five thousand miles."[129] Covering physical distance, in other words, and connecting far-flung buyers is as important as the volume of book sales. In fact, Ovington, white journalist, social worker, and cofounder of the National Association for the Advancement of Colored People (NAACP), builds her profile of Johnson around an explicit

---

[123] Ovington, "Selling Race Pride," 114. [124] Ibid., 113. [125] Ibid., 114.

[126] Mattern, "Fugitive Libraries," para. 6. [127] Ibid., para. 20.

[128] Carr, "We Must Seek on the Highways," 446.

[129] Ovington, "Selling Race Pride," 112.

recognition of the centrality of mobility and the road to bookselling. The profile begins with a novelistic scene of Johnson driving on, according to a local, "the wo'st road in the wo'ld":

> Mud! Mud! Mud! The little Ford coupe looks like a huge cake of red-clay dough. It jumps along the rough road like a chicken with its head cut off. The ruts are so deep that a truck has been caught in them and remains there, but the Ford, sliding and tumbling about, nevertheless goes ahead.[130]

The material pitfalls of the road – the mud and ruts – provide a metaphor for the racist challenges and resistance that impede a Black bookseller traveling through the southern states of the United States in the 1920s. Yet the Ford maneuvers, "sliding and tumbling" its way through. Its mobility – a metonymic extension of Johnson's own mobility – is undaunted and ultimately, triumphant.

Indeed, mobility is the operative dynamic in Johnson's profile. In a speech to Black churchgoers in Montclair, New Jersey that Ovington transcribes, Johnson begins by claiming her own mobility: "I went over to France with the YMCA, the only organization that sent colored women to the colored soldiers."[131] And Ovington herself tells of how she continues her interview of Johnson while they drive: "As we drive back in the little coupe to Newark after the church service I congratulated Miss Johnson upon her extraordinary success."[132] Feminist scholars such as Virginia Scharff and Alexandra Ganser have shown the contentious history of women's rights in the context of cars and driving.[133] As Nelles experienced five decades before, the road and its vehicles are "identified with masculinity and male mobility."[134] In Johnson's own travels and in Ovington's foregrounding of the road and driving, Johnson resists these socio-spatial dynamics and emphasizes her right to the road and mobile activism.

---

[130] Ibid., 111.   [131] Ibid., 112.   [132] Ibid., 113.

[133] Scharff, *Taking the Wheel*; Ganser, *Roads of Her Own*.

[134] Scharff, *Taking the Wheel*, 166.

Yet as a Black woman on the road, Johnson was subject to additional restrictions on mobility and access. The historical experience of space for Black Americans is one of confinement. From the captivity of the slave quarter to the separation and containment of racial segregation to the carceral state and red-zoned neighborhoods, the free mobility of Black Americans has been controlled by political, economic, legal, and social forms of whiteness. In the twentieth century, public vehicles of mobility, including trains and buses, were the targets of increased surveillance and restrictions for Black men and women. With the rise of automobile culture, car ownership promised a means for Black Americans to escape these restrictions and resist racial hierarchies, but also inspired new forms of policing and controlling mobility.[135]

While Johnson's car gave her the autonomy and necessary means to pursue her bookselling project, the roads were never free.[136] Historian Kathleen Franz explains that as white travelers imbued the open road with democratic value and access, "they simultaneously limited access to automobility through a system of discrimination and representation that positioned nonwhites outside the new motor culture."[137] For Black Americans, the roadmap was overlaid with a web of spatial exclusion

---

[135] Carr, "We Must Seek on the Highways," 446–447.

[136] To be sure, itinerant booksellers never roamed entirely freely. Restrictions on bookseller's mobility have been defined not only by gender and race but also by practical demands of the business. As book historian Ronald J. Zboray notes, these demands included finding a large enough customer base of buyers who could afford the books, taking advantage of established local patterns of gathering such as market days, election days, and church dedications, and setting up accessible deliveries of stock and ordered books. In addition to the demands of the trade, efforts to legally circumscribe the movements of itinerant booksellers became increasingly common by the mid-nineteenth century. Local licenses and ordinances required book agents to register and pay a fee; store booksellers, resentful of growing competition, reported agents. Zboray, *A Fictive People*, 42; Hackenberg, "The Subscription Publishing Network," 62; Jaffe, "Peddlers of Progress," 531.

[137] Franz, "The Open Road," 135.

woven by white supremacy. "The space of the American road, like the contours of citizenship," asserts Cotton Seiler, "was established under specific regimes of racialized inequality and limited access whose codes it reproduces."[138] That layered racial and racist geographies underlie America's roads was the foundation for the popular *Negro Motorist Green Book*, which began publication in 1936, four years after Johnson ended her bookselling career, and continued until 1967.[139] The *Green Book* included addresses of businesses that welcomed Black travelers. Acting as an alternative map for Black Americans on the road, the *Green Book* charted a path that avoided spaces of harassment and potential violence, including so-called "sundown towns" that prohibited Black people after dusk, and worked to facilitate African-American geographical mobility and spatially resist white supremacy.

Although the road has always been a potentially risky place for itinerant booksellers – from the threat of accidents and inclement weather to local restrictions and attitudes toward itinerancy – its racist exclusions presented heightened perils for Johnson and other Black booksellers. In the summer of 1930, bookseller Lorenzo Johnston Greene and four peers from Howard University left Washington, D.C. in a Model A Ford to sell books on African-American life and history published by the Association for the Study of Negro Life and History.[140] Greene recorded his experiences in a diary that was later edited by Arvarh Strickland, the first Black faculty member at the University of Missouri, and published in 1993. The racialized space of the road is established early in Greene's diary when he notes an "enjoyable ride through historic Fredericksburg [VA], where remains the only slave auction block in the United States."[141] The explicit noting of the site of the slave auction block highlights how Black Americans map a spatio-historical itinerary shaped by race, violence, and captive mobility.

In addition, Greene was aware of the active threats that might imperil the Black driver. He remembers,

---

138 Seiler, *Republic of Drivers*, 107. 139 Green, *Negro Motorist Green Book*.
140 Greene, *Selling Black History*, 2. 141 Ibid., 20.

> On the way to Suffolk [VA], I picked up two white men who
> hailed me for a ride as I was going across the James River
> Bridge. Unthinking of the hazard, I picked them up. [. . .] It
> was only after I had admitted them that I felt the imbecility
> of giving them a ride. So many tales of violence done to
> sympathetic motorists had reached my ears.[142]

These hitchhikers continued on their journey with gratitude to Greene. Nevertheless, the stories of racial violence that travel along these same byways create a new map layer that guides Greene's interactions and interpretations of his experiences on the road. Later, he describes seeing white men carrying guns on the side of the road in Alabama and notes how his driving partner "bends, anticipating shot."[143] When the booksellers enter Atlanta, Georgia, Greene mentions that their interactions with white people on the road from Nashville, Tennessee, to Atlanta were "exceedingly cordial" and they "were overwhelmed with kindness."[144] That Greene notes this is itself testament to a heightened awareness of racialized road space and an expectation of the opposite reception. A few paragraphs later, however, the specter of racial violence rises again, when Greene explains that Atlanta was "still agog" over the murder of a Black college student by a group of white men, and following the sentencing of one of the men to fifteen years in prison, the local Black community was bracing for continued violent reprisals.[145]

While Kathryn M. Johnson had firsthand experience of racial violence years before at an Arkansas college, her memoirs don't often mention dangers on the road.[146] However, one brief, but notable, confrontation with southern white police officers offers insight not only into how she

---

[142] Ibid., 39. [143] Ibid., 96. [144] Ibid., 85. [145] Ibid., 86–87.

[146] I am indebted to Jane Greenway Carr and her article "'We Must Seek on the Highways the Unconverted': Kathryn Magnolia Johnson and Literary Activism on the Road" for information on Johnson's unpublished memoirs, currently housed in the Kathryn M. Johnson Papers in Schlesinger Library at Radcliffe College. In the fall of 1906, Johnson, then a dean at Shorter College, a historically Black college in North Little Rock, Arkansas, sheltered Black

encounters the racialized road, but also how she uses her position as a bookseller to navigate and renegotiate forms of cultural authority. Driving near St. Petersburg, Florida, in 1926, Johnson describes being pulled over by white police officers. Interested in her New York State license plate, the officers question Johnson and her traveling companion, Ezella Mathis Carter, a beautician who sold hair products on the road and often traveled with Johnson. "I showed them I had only books," Johnson remembers. But the officers remain skeptical: "Guess we'll just take you on down to the jail – hard on your folks down here – what you doin' down here anyway?"[147] It takes an intervention from Carter to convince the police to let the women resume traveling. The officers' repeated indications of "here"—it's "hard on your folks down here" and "what you doin' here"—rhetorically establish a geography of belonging and exclusion. "Here" is not for Johnson and Carter as two Black women; "here" is an enclosed and regulated space. The threat she faces, then, is twofold. Johnson is forbidden both to be still – to be "here" – and to move through – to continue traveling "there."

As a strategy to escape this threatening enclosure, Johnson's assertion that she "had only books" is revealing in its disavowal of the radical potential of books as tools of resistance. Carrying "*only* books" positions the books as something harmless and unobjectionable to the police. A clever sleight of hand and an intentionally ironic one since the books she carries are specifically designed to undermine the racist hierarchies of knowledge and history that empower white authority structures, including law enforcement. As Johnson herself explains in her memoirs, the books on the two-foot shelf in her backseat "were selected with the desire to offset the silence of textbooks and other books regarding the achievement of colored people."[148] Her books speak out; they *articulate* – both discursively through their content and spatially as they stitch together communities of Black readers. But they must remain quiet, "*only* books," in this situation. Likewise, Johnson minimizes her own cultural work. In order to traverse

students and community women and children during the week-long Argenta race riot. Carr, "We Must Seek on the Highways," 447.

[147] Qtd in Carr, "We Must Seek on the Highways," 449. [148] Ibid., 444.

the racialized space of the American road as a Black woman bookseller, Johnson both asserts and disavows the transgressive potential of books, reading, and bookselling.

If Annie Nelles found bookselling on the road to be a space to claim agency over her own life and write her own story, for Johnson, itinerant bookselling allows her to revise the past and future of Black Americans. In her travels across the American South, with the steady ticking up of her speedometer, Johnson ties her own spatial mobility to the social mobility of the Black community. Her physical mobility thus carries a "burden of meaning" that "jumps scale" from the physical street map.[149] Johnson's two feet of "books that all the colored people ought to read" included volumes of W.E.B. DuBois, Carter Woodson, James Weldon Johnson, and Paul Lawrence Dunbar, children's books, as well as her own co-authored memoir of her experiences in France: *Two Colored Women with the American Expeditionary Forces*.[150] Her bookselling stock was driven by her mission to "sell race pride." Johnson, in fact, is deliberate in distinguishing her book-selling from that of the general book peddler: "I'm not first of all selling books," Johnson tells Ovington as they drive away from a successful sale at the Montclair, NJ, church. "I am first of all creating the desire to read a certain kind of book." "I want to sell books," she continues, but "Most of all I want to sell race pride."[151] For Johnson, the car is only one vehicle; the books are the essential vehicle for mobilizing community pride, a shared history, and an alternative future.[152] Bookselling is the key to progress and group advancement through supporting communal awareness of the historical, cultural, and intellectual contributions of African-Americans.

To facilitate race pride and its accompanying social advancement through sales of her books, Johnson traces and connects the local spatial nodes of Black community life in her southern bookselling travels. Over a century earlier, Parson Weems lauded the bookselling potential of wealthy cotton market towns in a letter to Carey.[153] For Weems and

---

[149] Cresswell, *On the Move*, 6–7.   [150] Ovington, "Selling Race Pride," 112.

[151] Ibid., 113.   [152] McHenry, "Reading and Race Pride," 493.

[153] Qtd in Zboray, *A Fictive People*, 41, Letter from Weems to Carey, October 15, 1796.

other southern book peddlers who found bookselling success in Southern cotton towns, it was the exploited labor of Black bodies in cotton fields that provided the material wealth for book buying. Johnson, however, maps an alternative geography of bookselling, one focused on the local nodes of Black churches and their rich community life.[154] As literary historian Elizabeth McHenry has argued, in order to access and understand Black American literacy practices and cultures one must look beyond traditional – white-constructed – institutions and spaces to more informal print and reading spaces, including community organizations and groups.[155] From the backseat of her Ford coupe along the American roads to the pulpits of local churches and in the books she sells by, about, and to Black Americans, Johnson reinforces social relationships and social identity across space, explicitly creating a new geography of belonging that aimed to incorporate Black Americans.

3.2 The Sidewalk Bookseller: Sites of Exchange

If itinerant booksellers claimed the road to facilitate multiple forms of mobility – physical, social, and cultural – the sidewalk vendor asserts the right to stay still, to *occupy* street space. From Singapore to Mumbai to Johannesburg to New York City, on folding tables or stacked boxes or cloths laid over pavement, booksellers carve entrepreneurial opportunity out of the contested space of the sidewalk. Sidewalk book vendors operate on a spectrum of formalization. With a history of over four hundred years of street bookselling from their distinctive green boxes along the stone quays of the Seine, Paris' well-known bouquinistes hold five-year licenses granted by city hall.[156] In Lahore, Pakistan, the weekly Anarkali book bazaar, in operation for over fifty years, remains an informal marketspace. Each Sunday on a service street in front of the famous Pak Tea House, book vendors display hundreds of secondhand books on clear plastic sheets, piled against walls, stacked on wooden tables, and weighing

---

[154] Ovington, "Selling Race Pride," 113.

[155] McHenry, *Forgotten Readers*, 10–11.

[156] Ratkovic, *La légend des Bouquinistes*; Henley, "Through Gilets Jaunes."

down handcarts.[157] In Morocco, Rabat and Casablanca's sidewalk book-sellers are distinguished by their material spaces. Bouquinistes sell books and print materials from U-shaped boutiques in souqs and medinas, while kiosquiers run open booths extending into the street, and terrassiers spread their books, newspapers, and magazines on the sidewalk.[158]

As "interstitial urban spaces," sidewalks support the mundane functions of urban life, including transportation, utilities, and waste removal.[159] At the same time, sidewalks operate as social, political, and economic spaces. Like the road, the sidewalk is both a material space and a social construct. For Jane Jacobs, who called sidewalks "the main public places of the city" and its "most vital organs," the social functions of the sidewalk – the street vendors, the playing children, the impromptu physical and conversational interactions – foster the cohesiveness needed for livable urban spaces.[160] Amid growing efforts to order and control the city's streets and sidewalks, Jacobs called for recognition of how the "intricate sidewalk ballet" of human activity creates safety and community in neighborhoods.[161] The diverse activities and the web of social, economic, and administrative uses, in other words, create the sidewalk, which in turn shapes urban life. As geographer Sig Langegger argues, the sidewalk is less a physical space than a process.[162]

At stake in this production of sidewalk space is the who, what, when, where, and how of it all. Who gets to use the sidewalk? How and in what ways? When can certain populations traverse the sidewalk and do all people have equal access to all of the sidewalk? As a mixed use space, the public sidewalk is constrained by an array of formal regulations, including build-ing, land use, and health codes, licenses, and parking policy.[163] In addition, multiple social groups negotiate conflicting interests and access to sidewalk

---

[157] "Gem in the Dirt"; Fatima, "Lahore's Sunday Book Bazaar."

[158] Cohen, "The Distribution of Knowledge."

[159] Kim, "The Mixed-Use Sidewalk," 226; Langegger, *Rights to Public Space*, 118–119.

[160] Jacobs, *The Death and Life*, 38.   [161] Ibid., 57.

[162] Langegger, *Rights to Public Space*, especially Ch. 6.

[163] Langegger, *Rights to Public Space*, 119.

spaces, from municipal bureaucrats to property owners to street vendors to political activists to the unhoused.[164] And power is distributed unevenly among these groups. A precarious economic practice, street vending is most often conducted by marginalized groups for whom forms of difference – socioeconomic, racial, religious, and nationality – mediate their relationship to street space. Conflict is thus not simply about uses of space, but about sociopolitical structures that create geographies of inclusion and exclusion. Sidewalk booksellers everywhere must erect their tables on and navigate the unstable and shifting boundaries of the sidewalk as regulated and politicized public and social space.

However, within this struggle over who owns, occupies, and manages sidewalk space, street booksellers inscribe new geographies of belonging. Invoking de Certeau's spatial tactics and Asef Bayat's "quiet encroachment" in which "ordinary people" gradually but insistently advance "on the propertied and powerful," Kristina Graaff and Noa Ha argue that street vendors create an inclusive space to "claim access to opportunities and public space that state-sanctioned constraints would deny them."[165] In setting down a table to engaging with passersby to forming relationships with brick-and-mortar businesses, street booksellers claim access and "give force to relations of belonging and inscribe regimes of territoriality."[166] Even if formal structures of belonging – legal regulatory structures or local business organizations – would seek to exclude the sidewalk bookseller, these practices of belonging reclaim and create space.

As a global phenomenon, sidewalk bookselling functions everywhere in tension with control of public space; however, local contexts of social, economic, and legal frameworks shape the specific forms and dynamics of bookselling practices.[167] The below discussion focuses on the local contexts of sidewalk bookselling in New York City. There, sidewalk booksellers have benefited from exemptions in street vending regulations for First Amendment print material. Nevertheless, municipal space management

---

[164] Loukaitou-Sideris et al., *Sidewalks*, 6.
[165] Graaff and Ha, "Introduction. Street Vending," 7.
[166] Langegger, *Rights to Public Space*, 118.
[167] Kim, "The Mixed-Use Sidewalk," 229–230.

strategies have attempted for over three centuries to circumscribe and contain street vending spaces, forms, and practices. Within this tension, New York City's sidewalk booksellers have created and negotiated their own geographies of belonging. From strategies to evade regulatory enforcement to the cultivation of intellectual exchange to the very books they sell, New York City's sidewalk booksellers use the liminal and contested space of the sidewalk not only to make a living but also to create an inclusive space that incorporates the book and bookselling into the dynamics of urban social exchange.

3.2.1 Claiming the Sidewalk

On July 4, 2016, police officers seized Kirk Davidson's books from his ten folding tables on the sidewalk of Broadway near 73rd Street on the Upper West Side. Joking that the July 4th date of the seizure made it an "American story," Davidson prepared to go back to court. No stranger to the legalities layered on his sidewalk space after thirty years as a sidewalk bookseller, by 2016, Davidson reported receiving nearly 200 summonses.[168] Regulating public space and peddling has a long history in New York City, nearly as old as the city itself. In 1691, to appease merchants in the public markets, street selling was prohibited until two hours after the markets opened.[169] And with the rise of the ideal of rationalized urban space, expressed in the planned right angles and gridded streets of the Commissioner's Map of 1811 and the rise of dedicated and specialized commercial establishments in the nineteenth century, the city was reordered for economic gain and the street and sidewalk revalued for smooth transit and traffic flow.[170] This shift, according to historian Daniel Bluestone, "anticipated not only the eradication of street buying and selling but also the eclipse of earlier social uses of the street for political activity, gregarious socializing, and popular amusements."[171] While the ubiquitous wooden wheeled pushcarts of immigrant communities on the Lower East Side drew the most regulatory

---

[168] Kilgannon, "A Sidewalk Vendor," para. 11.

[169] Bluestone, "The Pushcart Evil," 69.

[170] Ibid., 70; Bridges and Maverick, *This Map of the City of New York*.

[171] Bluestone, "The Pushcart Evil," 69.

attention in the late-nineteenth century, as the twentieth century progressed, the growth of urban planning, Manhattan real estate values, and population density refocused regulation on combating congestion.

As the regulatory gaze surveilled Manhattan's streets, the number of sidewalk booksellers grew, due in large part to their special status among street vendors. Afforded constitutional protections of free speech under the First Amendment, vendors of "newspapers, periodicals, books, pamphlets or other similar written material" are exempt from licensing requirements.[172] The New York City Council confirmed this exception in 1982, noting "that it is consistent with the principles of free speech and freedom of the press to eliminate as many restrictions on the vending of written matter as is consistent with the public health, safety and welfare."[173] Not required to obtain expensive licenses or to engage with labyrinthine licensing and renewal processes, more and more vendors set up sidewalk book and magazine tables.[174] According to the advocacy organization Street Vendor Project, in 2006 28 percent of downtown Manhattan street vendors were First Amendment vendors, though without a license requirement specific numbers remain difficult to calculate.[175]

However, although First Amendment vendors are afforded special consideration, they are subject to other regulations, primarily focusing on the space they occupy. For instance, a book vendor's stand can be no more than 3 feet wide and 8 feet long, cannot lean against a glass window, or be set up within a subway entrance, bus stop, driveway, or crosswalk.[176] In addition, First Amendment vendors, with the exception of U.S. military veterans, must also abide by the specific street restrictions for general vendors. This growing list of restricted streets works to corral vendors and reduce access to streets with highest pedestrian density, precisely what vendors need to sustain business.[177]

For sidewalk booksellers, as with other vendors, regulatory structures reflect in part the interests of established merchants concerned with

---

[172] "The Regulation of Street Vendors"; "Street Vending."
[173] Qtd. in "The Regulation of Street Vendors." [174] "Pushcart Wars."
[175] *Peddling Uphill*, 7. [176] *Peddler Handbook.*
[177] "20-465 Restrictions on the placement"; "FAQ."

competition from informal markets. In a historical example of the clash between formal and informal print markets, the publishing industry paper *The Newsman* reported in 1891 on a proposal from a group of local businessmen for erecting glass and iron kiosks on street corners from which to sell news and books.[178] The American News Company (ANC), which dominated the print distribution market, objected, arguing that the kiosks would be an economic disruption since they would unfairly compete with store-bound book and print dealers and reduce taxable property values. The proposal faltered when the ANC threatened to buy out all of the kiosks themselves.

The right to the sidewalk remains an economic power struggle. Today's Business Improvement Districts (BIDs), which became "a significant political force" in the 1980s, take up the economic and physical regulation of sidewalks, participating in the semi-privatization of urban space.[179] "Publicly authorized, legally sanctioned, privately administered institutions," BIDs are formed by local property owners for the ostensible purpose of protecting and boosting local business interests.[180] But "business interests" is a large and vague purview, and BIDs can be both aggressive in what they consider to be "protecting" business and limited in how they define "business." Street vendors, not considered businesses, are primary targets of BIDs, often in the name of neighborhood beautification or quality of life initiatives. Although the law does not expressly give permission to BIDs to regulate public space in their districts, urban planner Ya-Ting Liu notes that "BIDs have successfully extended their supplemental beautification efforts into a larger lobby for more restrictive policies toward street vendors."[181] From hiring security to installing planters or trees to lobbying the City Council, BIDs mold public sidewalk space.

Embedded in arguments about the economic implications of sidewalk vendors for businesses is the neoliberal urban ideal of ordered, unobstructed public space. The increase in book vendors in the 1980s and early 1990s as a result of First Amendment protections made them particularly visible targets for these arguments.[182] Peter Malkin, the chairman of a prominent

---

[178] "Do We Want Kiosks?" 2. [179] Duneier, *Sidewalk*, 232.
[180] Liu, "Right to Vend," 29. [181] Ibid., 30–31. [182] "Pushcart Wars."

BID, wrote in a 1992 *New York Times* editorial that sidewalk booksellers
contribute to "a sense of disorder" and "cause sidewalk congestion."[183]
Book vendors should be moved instead, he argues, "to restricted zones"
enforced by hired BID security so that they might "give our busiest sidewalks back to pedestrians." There is no acknowledgment of overlapping
geographies – that these pedestrians are also customers for sidewalk book
tables. In this spatial formulation, "restricted zones" recall efforts to create
bounded markets that contain and attempt to formalize informal street
markets and that recast sidewalks as neutral transit sites connecting nodes
in a formal economic geography of established stores.

This logic is tied to larger patterns of gentrification and global capital
flow into New York City, which demand "neoliberal landscapes of carefully
choreographed consumption, tourism, and entertainment that maximize the
value of property."[184] As one sidewalk bookseller noted, rising residential
and commercial rents in his area precipitated increased enforcement of
vending restrictions.[185] Graaff notes that disadvantaged neighborhoods in
Harlem, the Bronx, and Brooklyn face "less scrutiny" than valued areas of
Manhattan, "at least, until city planning shifts its attention to
a neighborhood's 'potential' for gentrification."[186] In response to Malkin's
complaints of disorder and congestion, Mark Solof, a street seller of used
books on the Upper West Side, asserted the book as a form of resistance to
this spatial ideal. "Mr. Malkin and his allies," Solof writes,

> are willing to sacrifice the operations of street booksellers
> throughout Manhattan – and in doing so, the lovely
> exchange of ideas in printed form – for the doubtful goal
> of achieving a sanitized environment in midtown that is akin
> to the environment of suburban malls and shopping
> districts.[187]

---

[183] "Book Vendors Shouldn't." [184] Devlin, "Street Vending," 44.
[185] Kilgannon, "A Sidewalk Vendor." [186] Graaff, "Ethnic Contestations," 119.
[187] "Let's Look Closer."

Street booksellers, then, operate "on the front lines" of community resistance to gentrification by visibly and physically asserting an alternative model of urban sidewalk space.[188]

This conflict over control of sidewalk space is expressed in the spatialized language used to define the book vendors' presence. In editorials, news articles, and public records, critics of sidewalk booksellers use the terms "encampment," "obstruction," "occupation," "clogged," and "virtual blockade," suggesting that the spatial logic of movement and flow is impeded by the stacked tables of booksellers.[189] In support of smooth transit through the city, which underpins formal capitalist enterprise and property valuation, this perception of public space means that city sidewalks must be made empty. The "crime of the hawker," Jonathan Anjaria argues, "is to contradict this dream."[190] He sets up a stand and stays, a rock in the flow of pedestrians, redirecting the current of the street into the eddies and stopped pools of his own entrepreneurial space. The language of street booksellers and their supporters echoes this alternative spatial logic by emplacing the bookselling stands. Variously labeled "an institution," "a fixture," "an open-air bookstore," "a metropolitan refuge," even a "funky haven," the sidewalk *IS* a bookselling space, not simply an empty stage on which illicit bookselling is performed.[191] Rhetorically emplacing the sidewalk book table physically claims the right to the city's sidewalks and resists the larger spatial dynamics of economic and social colonization.

Claiming space, of course, is more than a declaration of words; sidewalk booksellers also employ local spatial practices to emplace themselves. Informal strategies for managing space, for instance, focus on avoiding conflict with municipal authorities. In the West Village in 1992, sociologist Mitchell Duneier describes how sidewalk booksellers claimed specific corners. Muhammad and his family sold Black books and incense on the corner

[188] Naison, "Street Vending," 220.

[189] Kilgannon, "A Sidewalk Vendor"; Fein, "The Media Business," Duneier, *Sidewalk*, 235, 237.

[190] Anjaria, "Street Hawkers," 2142.

[191] Kilgannon, "A Sidewalk Vendor"; "Let's Look Closer"; Bergmann, "NYPD Again"; West Side Rag article; Duneier, *Sidewalk*, 319.

of 8th Street and 6th Avenue; further down the block, an older white man stocked bestsellers and hardcovers on the weekend.[192] Across the avenue at Greenwich Street were comics, and Alice, a Filipina woman, sold best-selling paperbacks. The "unofficial system" for adjudicating space disputes was "orderly" because, in Duneier's analysis, "it maximized the interests of vendors, whose method of allocating space had depended on minimizing contact with the official law."[193]

However, the passage of Local Law 45 in 1993 shifted this spatial management system. Stipulating that First Amendment vendors were restricted from the same streets where food and general vendors were already banned, the law dramatically reduced the vending space of book-sellers in the West Village. Disputes over available space increased, and a job category in the informal sidewalk vendor market, the "place holder," assumed a new role and significance. Often unhoused men who lived on the street, place holders would guard a specific location overnight, usually at the behest of the vendor. But shrinking vending space created new competition for sidewalk yardage and, as Duneier explains, place holders increasingly operated independently to demand payment for "reserving" or moving from an available vending location.[194] "I need a little space" became the focal point of negotiation on the sidewalk, and new systems for determining spatial rights emerged.[195] Even still, these informal spatial mechanisms sought to avoid direct conflict with law enforcement.

On the other hand, for at least one sidewalk bookseller, the increase in regulatory oversight and ever-multiplying subsections of municipal vend-ing ordinances presented its own opportunity for resistance. Kirk Davidson, the Upper West Side bookseller mentioned above, made a business out of

---

[192] Duneier, *Sidewalk*, 19.   [193] Ibid., 239–240.   [194] Ibid., 238–244.

[195] Ibid., 245. Duneier also discusses how the spatial restrictions of Local Law 45 also impacted the print matter sold on the streets. The seizure of new books from any vendor who happened to set up outside the boundaries for vending would often put the vendor out of business as he could not afford to replace his stock nor wait for the administrative processes to retrieve his goods. But vendors who sold scavenged or recycled items could more easily reestablish their business, prompting a shift in the print material for sale overall (250–252).

challenging his summonses. Through seizure and summons, and to the alternating frustration and support of neighborhood residents and businesses, Davidson returned each time, having paid the fine, or, more often, having the charge dismissed by citing administrative or enforcement errors.[196]

Contributing to his remarkable longevity was Davidson's familiarity with the municipal regulations for street vendors and book vendors more specifically. Following summons dismissals, the army veteran bookseller often sued the city for "unlawful enforcement and seizure." According to his own accounting, these suits have returned over $80,000. "That's what he lives off of," the city councilwoman for the area complains.[197] "It's a job in itself," Davidson explains, reframing the primary business of the street bookseller as resisting – and profiting off of – the overreaching regulatory oversight of urban space.[198] Rather than restricting his business, regulatory enforcement of urban space has itself become his business. In addition, Davidson has deftly turned racialized space to his own benefit. Street-level policing practices, such as stop-and-frisk and broken windows policies, disproportionately target Black and brown bodies. Since the street serves as sidewalk vendors' "income platform" and considering most sidewalk vendors are from marginalized groups, Davidson and other minority vendors face excessive law enforcement.[199] Yet as a result of Davidson's deft understanding of both his rights as a First Amendment vendor and the vagaries of administrative processes, the racialized surveillance and police action against him have instead contributed to his success and solidified his right to belonging on the street.

3.2.2 Sidewalks and Stories

In addition to the diverse ways that sidewalk booksellers deploy spatial strategies to claim a space for books and bookselling on the contested sidewalk, they also contribute to the dynamics of urban social exchange by opening alternative space for literary expression and book marketing. Harlem's streets and sidewalks, for instance, have long served as a space for

---

[196] Kilgannon, "A Sidewalk Vendor."   [197] Ibid.   [198] Ibid.
[199] Graaff and Ha, "Introduction," 6.

political protest through voice and print. As Mark Naison notes, Black activists and their allies, most notably from the 1910s to the 1940s, "claimed Harlem street corners as a space to expound radical philosophies from soapboxes and stepladders, sell newspapers and pamphlets on the streets and organize rallies and marches aimed at local injustices."[200] Prominent Black bookseller Lewis H. Michaux began his book business, one that would later become the African National Memorial Bookstore, from a street push cart in the early 1920s.[201] Street vending "by economically motivated immigrants and politically motivated activists" serves a central role in promoting ideas and organizing collective action.[202] This claiming of space for dialogue reflects bell hooks' assertion that "black folks equated freedom with the passage into a life where they would have the right to exercise control over space on their own behalf."[203] Over the following decades, the cascading impacts of anti-communism, fiscal crisis, a crack epidemic, and mass incarceration – alongside the regulatory frameworks discussed above – largely erased Harlem's street oratory and print vending spaces, with the exception of the main artery of 125th Street.[204]

But at the turn of the twenty-first century, a new genre of Black print began appearing on – and flying off of – the tables of Harlem's sidewalk booksellers. Focused on everyday life in contemporary urban settings, popular "street fiction" engaged the justice system, illicit economies of drugs and sex, racial biases, and hip-hop aesthetics.[205] The street served both as a plot structuring element within the narrative and as the primary means of marketing and distributing the books. In the early years, authors

---

[200] Naison, "Street Vending," 223. [201] Nelson, *No Crystal Star*, 44.

[202] Naison, "Street Vending," 230. [203] hooks, *Art on My Mind*, 147.

[204] Naison, "Street Vending," 227–230.

[205] Hill et al., "Street Fiction." The authors note several labels for this genre: street lit, hip-hop lit, ghetto fiction, and hip-hop fiction (76). It should be noted that there exists a long historical relationship between street selling and the development of print genres. Also termed "street literature" due to its location of sale and cheap accessibility to a broad reading public, broadsides, songsters, chapbooks, pamphlets, and prints and engravings, formed popular reading genres. See Atkinson and Roud, *Street Literature*.

often published independently and dealt directly with street vendors, creating an economy of books that operated outside of the traditional publishing and book market. As Kristina Graaff notes in her examination of the rise of the genre and its connection to West African immigrant and African-American sidewalk booksellers, the "exponential growth of the street literature selling business" from 2000 to 2005 "led to a comprehensive supply of popular African-American novels."[206] For one West African bookseller in Harlem, "books were selling like cake . . . I was selling cases, people were making lines at the stands."[207] This success allowed the bookseller to multiply his bookselling stands, establish a bookselling network of other West African book vendors, and uniquely, to enter the formal bookselling economy by opening a bookstore. As Graaff notes, the demand for street literature, due in large part to its ready availability on sidewalk tables, drove the expansion of the genre into thousands of titles and led to its commercialization. Sidewalk booksellers who entered the market after the initial boom years struggled in a saturated market.[208] Nevertheless, sidewalk vending, both in its earlier role in political activism and in its connection with street fiction, provided an inclusive and visible space for Black authorial voices that are often excluded from or marginalized in commercial publishing.

On tables across the city, sidewalk booksellers offer all types of books, from secondhand books to bestselling paperbacks to textbooks to out-of-print books to comic books, as well as a spectrum of print forms. Through the deliberate and opportunistic curation of their stock, whether through used-book donations, relationships with publishers and booksellers, or scavenging, sidewalk booksellers create spaces of community belonging and identity. The booksellers Duneier worked with in the West Village in the early 1990s specialized in different genres so that one might know which table to visit for which type of book.[209] Those who scavenge the recycling and refuse of the neighborhood for material to resell on sidewalk tables participate in the circulation of a neighborhood's reading tastes – reading

---

[206] Graaff, "Ethnic Contestations," 124–125.

[207] Qtd in Graaff, "Ethnic Contestations," 123.

[208] Graaff, "Ethnic Contestations," 125. [209] Duneier, *Sidewalk*.

neighborhood space through its reading materials. For Jen Fisher, who operates a sidewalk stand called VorteXity Books on Avenue A near St. Marks in the East Village, the neighborhood informs and is shaped by her stock in a different way. Her tables of deliberately curated books have "changed and been built by the people in the neighborhood."[210] Inquiries lead to new purchases; recommendations inspire other recommendations. A poet herself, Fisher stocks poetry, film and art books, literature and philosophy, and "any book that feels good." "The bookstand," she adds, "is a community project."[211]

Other sidewalk booksellers create community out of local conditions of absence through the books on their tables. Kurt Brokaw, a film critic for *The Independent*, Teaching Professor at The New School, and part-time sidewalk bookseller, sells rare and valuable twentieth-century paperbacks and pulp magazines at 80th and Broadway on the Upper West Side. Brokaw sees his sidewalk table as preserving space for a collector's market and community of specialty readers. With the decimation of Manhattan's general used and antiquarian book stores, his sidewalk table, he explains, is a "remnant" of "lost New York"—of the passing of a publishing industry and the loss of bookselling spaces for rare books.[212] In low-income parts of the city where high commercial rents coupled with discriminatory practices in small-business loans have discouraged independently owned bookstores, the sidewalk is *the place* for books.[213] Sidewalk vendors in these "bookstore deserts" offer oases to readers, giving communities access to books and the conversations and dialogue that are inspired by them.

It is these conversations enabled by sidewalk booksellers – the crafting of a participatory space of intellectual exchange – that are a final means through which sidewalk booksellers construct geographies of belonging. Though BIDs and regulatory structures attempt to constrain the entrepreneurial efforts of sidewalk booksellers, the street is not only an economic or legal space; it is also a social space. This was Jane Jacobs' focus: "The point of [. . .] the social life of city sidewalks is precisely that they are public. They bring together people who do not know each other in an intimate, private

---

[210] "Interview with a Bookseller." [211] Ibid.
[212] "PBO Noir Expert"; *The Booksellers*. [213] Graaff, "Ethnic Contestations," 126.

social fashion."[214] One young book buyer in the West Village explained his perception of the street book table and the bookstore through the lens of social exchange. Interviewed by Mitchell Duneier on his loyalty to Hakim Hasan's sidewalk book table of books on Black life, Jerome explains, "In the bookstore, they have a lot of arrogance. They have their Ph.D. or whatever their title may be, and they arrogant in a certain way. But at his table we could talk about the books."[215] Unlike the model of the "bookstore as home" discussed in the last section, for Jerome, the bookstore – coded by classism in his critique – is an elitist space. Rather, it's the public sidewalk book table that is an inclusive space for community-building. "You can talk to the vendor," Jerome continues, "because he sits there and he sees what goes on. He sees all that. And people talk to him more and relate."[216] For one street fiction bookseller, Graaff notes, "Discussions with or among his customers about topics, narrative strategies, or personal connections to the storylines are common at his table, making it a center of attraction as a public spot for meeting and debate."[217] Jen Fisher, the East Village VorteXity bookseller, calls these conversations "an intense chain of gathered knowledge." She compares sidewalk book conversations to the "oral tradition of storytelling: the movement of conversation and how it changes depending on the energy of the listener and the day."[218]

Pushing back against models of the sidewalk as transit and movement, or even about the sidewalk book table as simply a space of economic exchange, the book table is also a place to stop, to converse, to engage in the give and take of social exchange. Duneier adds, the "presence of books on the street tends to prompt discussions about moral and intellectual issues."[219] In sociologist Richard Sennett's formulation, a healthy urban public realm should entail sensory and bodily interaction; modern glass high-rises and car-centric planning largely eliminated these embodied interactions. The loss of social interaction and engagement among strangers contributed to "dead public space."[220] The street bookseller and his table, when figured as a participatory space of social and intellectual exchange, attempts to enliven

---

[214] Jacobs, *The Death and Life*, 62. [215] Duneier, *Sidewalk*, 31. [216] Ibid., 31–32.
[217] Graaff, "Ethnic Contestations," 123. [218] "Interview with a Bookseller."
[219] Duneier, *Sidewalk*, 25. [220] Sennett, *The Fall of Public Man*, 12.

and reanimate urban space as social space. Certainly, these exchanges and discussions can happen in a multitude of places, the bookstore included, as discussed in the first section, but more formalized spaces in general also come with, as Jerome's comments allude to, social practices or hierarchies based on class, race, and other factors that work against open access.

In New York City, ideals of intimate and participatory social contact are also tied to the spatial imaginary of the city. Defenses of sidewalk book vending regularly invoke its fundamental relation to the socio-spatial identity of New York City. "Sidewalk booksellers have long been part of the fabric of New York City," the *New York Times* acknowledges.[221] In Mark Solof's editorial opposing increased regulation of Upper West Side book vendors, he argues, "For New Yorkers, the restrictions will mean the loss of a feature of the city that, in however modest a manner, contributes to the atmosphere of intellectual exchange for which New York is renowned."[222] When Kurt Brokaw, the Upper West Side sidewalk dealer in vintage paperback and pulp fiction, is asked about his sidewalk book-selling and the "New York Scene," he notes, "Enough people walk up here once in a while that we can have some fun out here."[223] He identifies prominent figures that have stopped by his table, including author Philip Roth, journalist David Halberstam, and orchestra director James Levine, triangulating his sidewalk book table with the literary and cultural life of the city. Of actress Martha Plimpton, he notes, "she comes up here and she likes juvenile delinquency stuff. Where else can I have conversations like that except on the sidewalks of New York?"[224] The focus on walking – "walk up here" and "come up here"—as a means to experience urban space recalls de Certeau's spatializing act of creating the city by walking, as "*Wandersmänner*, whose bodies follow the thicks and thins of an urban 'text' they write."[225] In these formulations connecting sidewalk bookselling to an ideal projection of the city, sidewalk booksellers claim a right not only to the physical space of the city, but to its social and imaginary space as well.

---

[221] Kilgannon, "A Sidewalk Vendor." [222] "Let's Look Closer."
[223] "PBO Noir Expert." [224] Ibid.
[225] de Certeau, *The Practice of Everyday Life*, 93.

3.3 Reflection

Outside the bookstore, from behind tables on the sidewalks and traveling the roads by foot, cart, or car, street booksellers must negotiate competing claims to space. Experienced materially on local corners and roads, in local municipal courts and legal systems, and in abstract scales of international capital and social value systems, the tension between openness and control is a foundational socio-spatial dynamic of the street. Itinerant booksellers, especially those for whom the road was a precarious gendered and racialized space, navigated this tension and inscribed new boundaries through an insistent mobility often made possible by the cultural capital of the books they carried. For sidewalk booksellers, the point is to stay rooted, unmoved by the corralling of regulatory efforts, and to re-incorporate the book and bookselling into a model of the city as an inclusive space of dynamic social exchange. By expanding the geography of bookselling to include itinerant bookselling and the informal economies of sidewalk bookselling alongside bookstores, we might enrich our understanding of the ways that bookselling allows for self-creation, community formation, and geographies of belonging that resist formal structures of exclusion.

4 Pages: Navigating Bookseller Catalogues

This section moves to bookselling on the page by focusing on bookseller catalogues. As functional texts, bookseller catalogues support the market for books by advertising goods and facilitate the book trade by connecting distant readers and collectors with books. Book scholars and historians have traditionally used catalogues for valuable bibliographical information on provenance or to discern trends in the market.[226] But if we consider bookseller catalogues not as reference texts but as a material and discursive genre on their own, we can ask different questions about how catalogues are constructed, the forms they employ, and the ways in which these forms serve spatial and spatializing functions. Through such elements as covers, illustrations, and lists, bookseller catalogues shape practices of reading and browsing and, like other bookselling spaces, consolidate imagined social communities around book buying. In short, bookselling catalogues build the imaginative and social space of a bookstore.

On the title page of his No. 10 catalogue, issued in 1851, New York City bookseller William Gowans extolled the value of a book catalogue:

> Book Catalogues are to men of letters what the compass and
> the lighthouse are to the mariner, the rail-road to the
> merchant, the telegraph wires to the editor, the digested
> index to the lawyer, the pharmacopoeia and the dispensatory
> to the physician, the sign-post to the traveler, the screw, the

---

[226] Bookseller catalogues, while understudied as a genre, have been used for a variety of research purposes. See Taylor's, *Book Catalogues*; Pollard and Ehrman, *The Distribution of Books by Catalogue from the Invention of Printing to A.D. 1800, Based on Material in the Broxbourne Library*. Scholars in the decades since have expanded inquiries into catalogues as resources for research on book trades and the history of the book, methods of book marketing, the history of libraries, and intellectual and literary history. Several of these sources are cited in the next section. See also: der Weduwen, Pettegree, and Kent, *Book Trade Catalogues in Early Modern Europe*; Hooks, "Booksellers' Catalogues and the Classification of Printed Drama in Seventeenth-century England," 445–464; Raven, *The Business of Books*.

wedge, and the lever, to the mechanic; in short, they are the
labor-saving machines, the concordances, of literature.[227]

This quotation draws conspicuous attention not to the loftier ideals of
literary endeavor or the objects for sale, but rather, to the text in hand – the
catalogue. The piling metaphors draw comparisons between the booksellers' catalogue and communication and transportation technologies and
tools and materials of diverse trades, ultimately arguing for the catalogue as
the essential "machine" of literature.

But the metaphor I'd like to focus on is the one that opens the quotation
and is later repeated: the book catalogue as a tool of wayfinding. The
"compass and the lighthouse" guide the mariner to safe harbors and "the
sign-post" directs the traveler along the road as the book catalogue guides
and directs the book buyer and reader on their own journeys. This spatial
and geographic metaphor is extended on Gowans' title page with the
inclusion of a street map that directs buyers to his store at 178 Fulton
Street. "Gowan's Bookstore" is triangulated with the Astor House, the Park
Theater, Barnum's Museum, and St. Paul's Church. Plotting the bookstore
in a geography of well-known urban cultural landmarks, this map offers not
only a physical path to access the store but also a way to interpret its cultural
value. A few years later, when Gowans moved northeast a few blocks to
Centre Street near Worth Street, he included his shop among more humble
trade neighbors, such as a "clockmaker" and the Harlem Railroad Depot,
but also right next door to the notorious New York jail, the Tombs. These
two maps describe not only the different physical locations of Gowans'
stores, but also different associational geographies. Wayfinding is both
physical and symbolic in these maps. Associated with other buildings,
locations, and landmarks, wayfinding journeys through physical and symbolic geographies, engaging with the ways humans make meaning out of
space and place.

To take Gowans' metaphor seriously and explore the book catalogue as
a wayfinding genre, I draw together Kevin A. Lynch's urban design concept
of wayfinding and media scholar Johanna Drucker's "phenomenal book."

[227] William Gowans, *Gowans' Catalogue*.

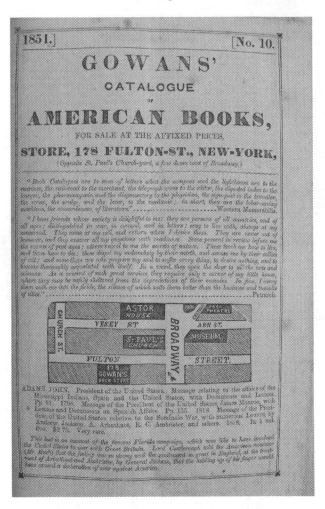

Figure 6 Cover. William Gowans, *Gowans' Catalogue* (New York, 1851). Photograph courtesy of the Grolier Club of New York.

Wayfinding, most broadly, is our ability to and process of finding our way. It is how we perceive and navigate space and place through the combination of physical elements in the landscape and our own mental maps.[228] The cognitive processes of wayfinding were first outlined in Lynch's 1960 book, *The Image of the City*. In order to plan a "legible city," or a city that utilizes the ways in which its residents construct cognitive maps, Lynch argues that planners must consider five specific elements core to human wayfinding: paths, edges, districts, nodes, and landmarks.[229] These elements layer the physical and symbolic, material and imaginative features and associations of the city and its spaces, highlighting wayfinding as both a physical act and a mental projection. In addition, the central use of "legible" in Lynch's formulation of the "legible city" highlights wayfinding as a reading act. The wayfinding individual must effectively read the city. Extending the link between urban and printed forms, Lynch compares the city as text to a page from a book: "Just as this printed page, if it is legible, can be visually grasped as a related pattern of recognizable symbols, so a legible city would be one whose districts or landmarks or pathways are easily identifiable and are easily grouped into an over-all pattern."[230]

If the city-as-text is constituted through the interaction and interpretation of the spatial elements of paths, edges, districts, nodes, and landmarks, then we might look to the constitutive elements of a book to understand wayfinding as a process of reading and making meaning in a book. Tables of contents, indices, and introductions, among other textual elements, structure the space of the book and guide the reader through its pages. This information architecture and other graphic forms act as spatial "navigational devices" that not only guide the reader materially through the book, but also allow for the interactive and embodied production of meaning. The text means nothing until we open it and engage. What do we emphasize? What and how do we learn? The ways in which readers interact with these elements – like wayfinding in physical space – create what Johanna Drucker terms the "phenomenal book."[231] "We make a work through our

---

[228] Golledge, *Wayfinding Behavior*, 6–7. [229] Lynch, *Image of the City*, 2–3.
[230] Ibid., 2. [231] Drucker, "The Virtual Codex," para. 14.

interaction with it," she argues. The "complex production of meaning and effect" is produced through "dynamic interaction" with the book.[232]

In considering bookseller catalogues as wayfinding genres, these structuring elements assume significant dimensions. On the one hand, they offer insight into how booksellers and readers navigate the material catalogue. In addition, considering Drucker's formulation, these elements are essential aspects in creating and perceiving meaning in and through the catalogue. I argue that attention to these structuring elements allow us to "read" the bookstore through the pages of the catalogue. They do more, in other words, than allow readers to identify what book to purchase or organize bibliographic information. Rather, through a reader's interaction with the structural elements of the text, the bookseller catalogue actively creates the meaningful space of the bookstore, guiding readers through real and imagined social and consumer spaces and shaping practices and values of reading and knowledge production.

Following a brief overview of the history and diverse forms of bookseller catalogues, I turn to specific structuring elements of catalogues, focusing on covers, illustrations, and the table of contents and index in order to explore how bookseller catalogues spatialize bookselling. Wayfinding, in addition to an interpretive framework, is also a methodological guide. It is necessarily exploratory, tracking one path while leaving aside alternatives. The below discussion focuses primarily on American book catalogues in the nineteenth century with some connections to twentieth-century conventions and examples. I hope to track a path through bookseller catalogues that is suggestive and illuminating, while also incomplete and selective and that allows for alternative paths and plotted points. Ultimately, by paying attention to bookseller catalogues as dynamic spatial forms, we might acknowledge the complex work of these seemingly mundane and functional texts.

4.1 The Bookseller Catalogue

Bookseller catalogues are a diverse genre, encompassing retail and wholesale book sales, dealers' catalogues, auction catalogues, and publishers'

[232] Ibid.

catalogues, with overlap among all of these categories. Additional book catalogues have been issued by circulating, institutional, and private libraries. The precise description of what makes a book catalogue is difficult to fix. It may be as simple as a "complete descriptive list" and take the form not only of a book or pamphlet, but also a broadside or advertisement in the back matter of a printed book.[233] With diverse changes in the nineteenth century, including the expansion of print, communication, and transportation networks, the rise of industrial production practices, and an emergent consumer economy, trade catalogues – a separate and often lengthy publication with detailed product and mail-order information – became an essential genre in promoting commerce. Antiquarian Don Fredgant, in *American Trade Catalogs*, defines a catalogue as

> printed broadsides, booklets, or books designed to engender business between the seller (the issuer of the catalog) and the buyer (the reader of the catalog), especially in the area of goods listed or described in the publications (catalogs). They may or may not be illustrated, may or may not contain actual process, and may be issued either by a manufacturer, a distributor (wholesaler), or a retailer.[234]

Despite this broad definition that emphasizes commercial purpose as the defining characteristic of a catalogue, Fredgant excludes auction catalogues as well as those for "secondary sales," thus leaving out the prolific trade and printing of used, secondhand, rare, and antiquarian bookseller catalogues.[235] So it's not precisely the purpose of a catalogue that defines the genre, since all of these catalogues are for the purpose of selling books; rather, it is its content or the specific (new) products for sale. For bibliographer Robert Winans, book catalogues can be categorized in three ways depending on format: "printed catalogues issued as separate entities; printed catalogues issued as part of a larger unit, such as those appearing as a section of a book or of a newspaper or periodical; and manuscript catalogues."[236] As

[233] Qtd in Fredgant, *American Trade Catalogs*, 17.

[234] Fredgant, *American Trade Catalogs*, 11. [235] Ibid., 30.

[236] Winans, *A Descriptive Checklist*, vii.

a genre, the catalogue is slippery, distinguished alternately by its form, content, or purpose.

Book catalogues are among the oldest of printed catalogue forms. In the 1460s and 1470s, booksellers in Mainz, Strasbourg, and Augsburg issued printed advertisements with descriptions for newly published works, most echoing earlier conventions for manuscript advertising.[237] Book historian Lotte Hellinga pins the earliest list advertisement to Mainz bookseller Peter Schoeffer, former apprentice of Johannes Gutenberg, who listed twenty-one titles for sale in 1469.[238] In 1484, Erhard Ratdolt of Venice issued his list of forty-six titles divided into the subject headings of Theology, Logic, Humanities and Poetry, Law, Astronomy and Geometry, and Medicine.[239] In what scholars consider the first book catalogue, fellow Venetian Aldus Manutius affixed prices to his 1498 printed broadside of Greek books.[240] And in 1537, Basel bookseller Johannes Hervagius and partners issued the first catalogue in booklet form.[241] Paris booksellers would do the same in the 1540s, issuing small booklets including information that would soon become conventional: author, short title, place of publication or sale, printer or publisher, and format. With the rise of international book fairs in Frankfurt and Leipzig, printed fair catalogues, organized by language and subject, offered a comprehensive overview of available published works.[242]

The idea of a central, authoritative book catalogue on the German model would never fully take hold in America. Frederick Leypoldt, later the founder of *Publisher's Weekly*, lamented this lack in an 1863 letter to the trade paper *American Publishers' Circular*:

> I soon felt, "very sadly" too, a deficiency of the book-seller's most indispensable tools – a well-supported central organ and–good catalogues. I wondered for long, how it was, that

---

237 Coppens and Nuovo, "Printed Catalogues," 146.
238 Hellinga, "Sale Advertisements," 9. 239 Hellinga, "Sale Advertisements," 14.
240 Coppens and Nuovo, "Printed Catalogues," 148; Maclean, "Book Sales Catalogs," 339.
241 Coppens and Nuovo, "Printed Catalogues," 149.
242 Maclean, "Book Sales Catalogs," 339–340.

in this country, where everything is offered to us so extremely practical and handy – especially timesaving tools and instruments – the booksellers have been neglected so much. I confess, I am a spoiled child in matters of book lists and catalogues, having been brought up in Germany – "the living catalogue of Europe!"[243]

We might note the final line: country as a catalogue; a catalogue as place. Fifty years before, in 1804, Boston booksellers had attempted a central catalogue, publishing a catalogue of 250 books printed in the United States in nine subject categories.[244] Yet despite various efforts to consolidate publication and bookselling information, book catalogues in America remained largely firm and bookseller-specific. Late-eighteenth- and nineteenth-century bookseller catalogues might range from a couple pages to a few hundred pages and be issued monthly, quarterly, or entirely irregularly. Some might focus primarily on a simple list of books, with perhaps a few descriptions interspersed, while others include extensive introductory material by the booksellers outlining their bookselling and literary philosophy, terms of sale, and copious book descriptions. In addition to printed catalogues that give more complete imprint listings but could be expensive and difficult to keep current, publishers and booksellers might list titles of available books on bills and correspondence or add lists or a full catalogue to popular publications like almanacs and periodicals.[245]

From the mid-to-late nineteenth-century and into the twentieth century, through the rise of the antiquarian book trade and collectors and dealers' markets, bookseller catalogues take diverse forms and subjects. They might focus on a specific historical period, author, genre, or theme, such as Randall House's *What Katy Did: A Recognition of Feminism in the American Experience* (2003) or The Jenkins Company's 1976 catalogue celebrating the bicentennial of the United States, which included at least

---

[243] Frederick Leypoldt, Letter to Editor of the APC, February 2, 1863, *Publishers Weekly* 25 (April 5, 1884): 443–444. Cited in Hruschka, *How Books Came*, 108.

[244] Growoll, *Book-Trade Bibliography*, 1. [245] Zboray, *A Fictive People*, 20.

one item from every year in the nation's history.[246] Catalogues might detail a personal collection or archive or even a single object. Book catalogues issued by a single firm can look remarkably consistent or wildly different. In one notable example British book dealer Simon Finch Rare Books Limited issued Catalogue 40 (1999), titled "Unchained," in the form of a deconstructed set of pages – an unbound book – contained in a color printed hardcover case.[247] The previous No. 39 catalogue used a solid cream-colored soft cover binding with the title "English Books to 1800" printed in simple, all-caps serif typography, reflecting historical print conventions and the content for sale.[248] As bookseller Don Lindgren notes, diverse influences and structural forces, including economic pressures and technological limitations, in addition to collection contents and bookseller aspirations, shape how booksellers create and distribute catalogues.[249] Large format, color illustration, or bound or avant-garde catalogues could be issued by established booksellers and dealers. Other booksellers rely on simpler list mailers. The rise of word processing and publishing software, as well as CD-ROM and portable document format (PDF), has diversified the formats, designs, and distribution methods of book catalogues.

4.2 Catalogue Covers

Consider that first moment of encounter with the catalogue, through a cover, wrapper, or title page.[250] This external announcement of the catalogue serves several purposes. Practically, it is an introduction to the

---

[246] Randall House, *What Katy Did: A Recognition of Feminism in the American Experience*. Catalogue no. 30. Santa Barbara, CA, 2003; The Jenkins Company, *American Celebration: The Creation and Evolution of the United States as Reflected in the Printed and Written Word, 1776-1976. Catalogue No. 100*. Austin, TX: 1976. Both catalogues included in Payne, *Great catalogues*, 319–320, 185–187.

[247] *Unchained by Simon Finch: Catalogue 40*. London: Simon Finch Rare Book, 1999.

[248] *English Books to 1800 Catalogue 39*. London: Simon Finch Rare Books, 1999.

[249] Beale, "Don Lindgren."

[250] Due to the variety of book parts discussed here, I use "cover" as shorthand for any external front of a catalogue. Specific variations are noted when relevant.

essential information of the bookseller and their offered books. As the first point of contact in a commercial interaction, the cover might attract interest through eye-catching layout, illustration, or color. Further, mediating the interaction between the bookseller and the reader of the catalogue, the cover dynamically shapes the reader's interpretation of the bookseller and the catalogue. As structuring elements of the page, content and design "have the potential," according to visual communication scholar Alison Barnes, "to develop the page and the book as spaces of interpretation" and "to undertake a performative role in the construction of the text."[251] More than simply a neutral or passive page of identifying information, covers, in other words, embody and act on meaning. Catalogue covers are a first element in creating the space in which books are sold, guiding the reader's interpretation of the bookseller and their catalogue.

Catalogue covers offer an opportunity to brand and shape the identity of the bookstore and bookseller. Sometimes this identity might be quite literal. Before Appleton & Company became an established and prominent publisher and bookseller in the 1850s and used only Appletons' or D. Appleton & Co. on their catalogue covers, their catalogues experimented with diverse bookstore identities. An 1835 catalogue highlighted the "D. Appleton & Co. Theological, Classical, and Miscellaneous Bookstore."[252] On an 1840 cover, they were the "European and American Bookstore," and in 1841, a catalogue cover advertised books "For Sale by D. Appleton & Co., at their Literary Emporium."[253] Each of these store titles posits a different identity. In other cases, bookseller identity might be shaped more indirectly. In the first half of the twentieth century, longtime New York book firm Charles Scribner's Sons became known for their colorful catalogue covers and wrappers showcasing specific collection themes. Scribner's catalogues emphasized the power of catalogues to define and pioneer collecting fields and to record and create cultural knowledge. Diverse cover designs alongside catalogue content helped accomplish this work.

---

[251] Barnes, "Geo/Graphic Design," 167.

[252] D. Appleton & Co., *Catalogue of an Extensive Collection.*

[253] D. Appleton & Co., *Catalogue of English Books, Modern Editions;* Appleton, D. & Co., *Catalogue of English Books in the Several Departments.*

Covers were colorful and simply designed, most often with only the content title and the bookseller listed. "Science and Thought in the 19th Century" announced a 1938 catalogue wrapper with bold white lettering on a vivid royal blue background; Catalogue 105 offered "First Editions of Famous American Songs" in black script type on textured tan paper. Later that year, Scribner's issued a catalogue on "First Editions of Juvenile Fiction 1814–1924" with a cover depicting the title and bookseller in black print on a white flagged background and black-and-white photographs of select children's books standing splayed with cover facing out.[254]

Of course, as printing and illustration technologies developed through the twentieth century, booksellers, and especially those specializing in art books or unique fields, also used covers in increasingly creative and evocative ways. Consider, for instance, the deluxe cloth cover of The Book Sail's (Orange, California) 1984 Anniversary Catalogue showcasing a printed red flame on black background with a 3-D portrait of Elvira with book and skull.[255] Or New York bookseller J. N. Herlin's 1984 catalogue on conceptual artist books, which used a clear pocket cover printed with an x-ray of Herlin's skull on the front and a photo portrait on the back. Once the catalogue contents were removed from the cover pouch, the two images were superimposed "to create an image reminiscent of medical schools' flayed anatomical figures."[256]

While unique and dynamic covers – especially those of rare book dealers – naturally attract attention and create bookseller recognition, even covers that seem to be simply an identification and description of

---

[254] Charles Scribner's Sons, *Science and Thought in the 19th Century: A Collection of First Editions. Catalogue No. 113.* New York: The Scribner Book Store, 1938. In Payne, *Great Catalogues*, 398–410; Charles Scribner's Sons, *First Editions of Famous American Songs;* Charles Scribner's Sons, *First Editions of Juvenile Fiction.*

[255] *Literature, Art and Artifacts That Will Forever Remain Among the Undead. 16th Anniversary Catalogue.* Orange, CA: The Book Sail, 1984. In Payne, *Great Catalogues*, 19–23.

[256] Jean-Noël Herlin, correspondence with Payne Associates, December 21, 2014. Qtd in Payne, 165; *Brain Storms. Catalogue No. 8.* New York: J. N. Herlin, 1983.

catalogue content shape perceptions of booksellers and books and describe geographies of the book trade. The covers of mid-nineteenth-century American catalogues, like the newspapers of the time, could be very busy places. And without the eye-catching art or vibrant colored covers that we now associate with dealers' catalogues, it is easy to read past the work they are doing. New York City bookseller T. W. Reeve crammed the cover of his November 1857 catalogue not only with the expected catalogue title, "A Descriptive and Priced Catalogue of a Collection of Valuable London Books, Just Imported from Europe" and bookseller name and location, but also with a 22 line block paragraph printed in small type detailing the ship on which the books arrived, the European book purchaser and general provenance of the imported books, sample titles, and an assurance that "none of the books in this catalogue were purchased of booksellers or dealers in waste paper."[257] Following this paragraph, which takes up about one-third of the cover page, appear assurances of low prices and high quality, a general return policy, an epigraph, and a directive to redistribute the catalogue to a "book-buying friend." At least fifteen different typefaces and sizes are used in this single cover page.

The Leggat Brothers, booksellers specializing in secondhand books, echoed this manic cover – both in content and in design – in their No. 42 catalogue.[258] However, instead of mapping the geography of books to bookseller, their cover includes a short paragraph on getting the books out through mail order costs and directions. The cover also advertises a list of eight additional Leggat Brothers catalogues on other genres, as well as discounts on bulk orders. Burnham Brothers of Boston issued their 1850 catalogue with a packed cover that incorporated an explanation of why and where one might need books into the title:

> Catalogue of Novels, Tales, Romances, Travels, Memoirs, Narratives, and other Miscellaneous Books, suitable for Circulating Libraries, or for Ship Libraries, or for companions to people who are about making long voyages, and

[257] T.W. Reeve, *No. 8. A Descriptive and Priced Catalogue*.
[258] Leggat Brothers, *Centennial Catalogue*.

Figure 7 Cover. T.W. Reeve, *No. 8. A Descriptive and Priced Catalogue* (New York, 1857). Photograph courtesy of the Grolier Club of New York.

want something amusing to relieve the tedium of the voyage, and beguile them of their weary moments.[259]

Considered together, each of these catalogues outlines geographies of books based on provenance, distribution, or reading, establishes specific hierarchies of information, and projects the space and values of the bookstore using cover content. Reeve stresses the source of his books and timeliness, claiming an authority through his European import connections. The Leggat Brothers, with their cover focus on mail order and price schemes, asserts the value of books as (affordable) commodities. And the Burnham Brothers just want the reader to be entertained on their journey; their cover foregrounds the act of reading. Each of these covers – though visually similar in design –offers distinctive interpretations of the space and purpose of books and shape the identity of booksellers and their stores.

4.3 Bookstore Illustrations

The development of woodcut, chromolithography, and photographic illustration in the nineteenth and early twentieth centuries led to a merging of image and text inside many trade catalogues. Historian Claire L. Jones notes that medical instrument companies included product images first through full-page plates in catalogues at the end of the eighteenth century and then as single images integrated with text descriptions by the 1860s.[260] Although nearly all bookseller catalogues in nineteenth-century America eschewed images of books, a number did include illustrations of bookstore spaces on catalogue front and back covers. Illustrations of exterior or interior views of the bookstore act as signposts guiding the reader into the imagined space of the bookstore through its pages. These images offer an additional dimension for thinking through the ways that catalogues act as a wayfinding genre, leading readers not only through the catalogue but also through imagined bookstore space and imagined communities of customer-readers. In their function as "traveling" salespeople, catalogues "represent the company of a human sales person, or they represent companies when the

---

[259] Burnham and Brothers, *Catalogue of Novels.*
[260] Jones, "Instruments of Medical Information," 571–573.

customer could not get to their stores."[261] Put another way, catalogues collapse physical and imaginative distance between the store and its customers. Images of bookstores that frame the catalogue invite readers into this real-and-imagined space.

Booksellers could deploy storefront images on their catalogues to consciously shape the ideals of a community. In his 1848 catalogue, New Yorker John Doyle plotted his "Cheap Ancient & Modern Book Store" at 146 Nassau Street as "the Moral Centre of the Intellectual World."[262] A cover vignette of the exterior of the store – interested more in making a statement than matching scale – depicts a Brobdingnagian bookstore with a window display of books dwarfing curious pedestrians who peer in the shop from the sidewalk and street. The outsized claim of being the "moral centre" appears on a signpost planted like a flag in the center of the image. Doyle's reorientation of the geography of intellectual life, while certainly a sales pitch carving a niche for the secondhand book market, also claims a specific philosophy on the value of books and bookselling. Locked in competition with new and larger booksellers on the commercial artery of Broadway a few blocks to the west, Doyle presents his bookstore as an alternative space where "literary pursuits" value the intellectual content of the recirculated secondhand text over the aesthetics of the new book as object. By offering a stylized image of his bookstore on the cover of his catalogue, he invites like-minded readers to enter that idealized space through the pages of the catalogue.

"Retail-scapes," according to historian Joanna Cohen, grew as a popular commercial genre in the nineteenth-century with the expansion of local and distant consumer cultures.[263] Images of storefronts, appearing on trade cards and billheads, in periodicals and in advertisements in books, could bridge scene and spectator and invite the viewer into the scene. When, for instance, Elizabeth Pierce arrived, tired and disoriented, to Concord, New Hampshire, in 1843, she glanced out of her hotel window and found comfort in a familiar storefront. "I recognized immediately the bookstore of John F. Brown," she wrote in her diary, "with wh[om] I had long been familiar,

---

[261] Fredgant, *American Trade Catalogs*, 9.   [262] John Doyle, *Part First*.
[263] Cohen, *Luxurious Citizens*, Chapter 5.

PART FIRST.

CATALOGUE

OF A

LARGE AND VALUABLE COLLECTION

OF

ANCIENT AND MODERN BOOKS,

IN EVERY DEPARTMENT OF

HUMAN KNOWLEDGE,

FOR SALE, AT EXTREMELY LOW PRICES FOR CASH, BY

JOHN DOYLE,

AT THE CHEAP ANCIENT AND MODERN BOOKSTORE,
THE MORAL CENTRE OF THE INTELLECTUAL WORLD,
NO. 146 NASSAU STREET, NEW YORK.

Figure 8 Cover. John Doyle, *Part First. Catalogue of a Large and Valuable Collection* (New York, 1848). Photograph courtesy of the Grolier Club of New York.

as engraven upon the cover of my pocket Almanak . . . It seemed like an old friend."[264] Pierce had formed a sympathetic relationship – a friendship – with Brown's bookstore solely through the familiar image of his storefront. Images of bookstores on the covers could thus create an affective geography, a sense of topophilia or love of place.[265] Pierce's mental, emotional, and cognitive ties to Brown's bookstore, mediated through the bookstore image, creates a sense of being "at home," allowing her to orient herself to a new place and providing access to an imagined community. When Kathryn Magnolia Johnson later posited that pictures of books in a catalogue won't sell – "You can't buy books from pictures, as you can dresses and farm implements" – she was focusing on selling specific book titles and content. Elizabeth Pierce's reflections highlight that a bookstore illustration is selling the store and its affective experience.

Images of the interiors of bookstores further an acclimatization process. Often appearing on the back covers of catalogues with the exterior view on the front cover, the depictions of bookstore interiors use the physical bookstore to frame the catalogue. In one 1893 catalogue issued by Philadelphia bookseller Edwin S. Stuart, owner of Leary's Bookstore, an engraving of the interior of the store on the back cover of the catalogue presents an active scene.[266] Imagined customers tarry in a functional space where architectural design is dominated by books. Books stretch the side margins, outlining the walls of the bookstore; vertical and horizontal book stacks lie on an open table display and several oversize folios and books are piled knee-high on the floor. While there are indications of commercial activity – a small cashier's desk tucked behind a center display with a single customer mid-purchase and a small sign lining the topmost bookshelf with directions on where to find the price of a book – the larger scene stresses literary engagement. Almost two dozen individuals are depicted, nearly all with a book in hand either reading or browsing the shelves. Reading is a solitary act, done alongside a floor display, shelf, or in a chair. Only a few customers, possibly customers and a clerk, engage in conversation. Considering these compositional details, the scene sanctions the role of

[264] Qtd. in Zboray and Zboray, *Literary Dollars and Social Sense*, 143.

[265] Tuan, *Topophilia*, 93. [266] *Leary's Old Bookstore*.

Figure 9 "Leary's Old Book Store" (Philadelphia, ca 1893). Collections of Library Company of Philadelphia.

the individual in navigating the bookstore and cultivating literary interests. The viewer-reader of the catalogue might shop alongside these imagined customers, selecting listed titles from their places on the bookshelf-pages and reading through descriptions.

These interior images, appearing on catalogues for other bookstores as well, model an array of consumer and social practices for book buying, shaping the catalogue-reader's conception of the bookseller and bookstore and the associations and acts of reading and buying books. Through their placement on the back covers of catalogues, with depictions of the exterior store on the front cover, the bookstore images enact the move from the external public face of the street to the internal intimate space inside the bookstore. Thus, the catalogue is refigured as a spatial experience in which readers browse the page-stacks of the bookstore, journeying through and reenacting the space of the bookstore by engaging with the pages of the catalogue.

Images of bookstores, especially on cover pages of catalogues, would become increasingly rare in the twentieth century, instead replaced by photography of book covers, title pages, bindings, and sample pages of listed books inside the catalogue. On occasion, photographs of shelved collections or some other visual representation of physical bookstore space might be included.[267] However, a corollary to the nineteenth-century catalogue covers depicting bookstores might be glimpsed in today's book-store websites, which are the contemporary means of collapsing the distance between bookseller and book buyer – physical site to virtual site, print page to webpage.[268] Photographs of store exteriors and interiors on these sites, like those on nineteenth-century catalogue covers, enable the formation of conceptual maps that facilitate wayfinding in a real-and-imagined bookstore by building familiarity with the physical space of the store and allowing the customer to project themselves within and navigate a local community of readers and book buyers.

4.4 Table of Contents and Index

Once we've entered the bookstore-as-catalogue, a variety of other forms and content direct our paths and shape the knowable space of the bookstore, from the table of contents to subject headings to editorial interjections.

---

[267] Catalogue No. 19 *Americana: Books, Pamphlets, Early Voyages*, issued in the early 1840s to advertise the George W. Soliday Collection of Western Americana, included a frontispiece with a photograph depicting the exterior of the Soliday's home library. The accompanying caption acts as an invitation inside: "View of the rear of the George W. Soliday library, facing Lake Washington. The entrance door is behind the chair in the right foreground. The late Mrs. Soliday stands overlooking her garden." Included in Payne, p. 56–59.

[268] Many brick-and-mortar bookstores with a website could be included as evidence. A random sampling: The Writer's Block in Anchorage, Alaska, https://writers blockak.com/; Subterranean Books in St. Louis, Missouri, https://store .subbooks.com/; Bad Animal Books in Santa Cruz, CA, www.badanimalbooks .com/.

A catalogue, like any book, is made up of a variety of structuring elements – "dynamic scaffolding" in Joanna Drucker's words – that shape and guide engagement with the text.[269] Illustrations, as discussed above, are one element, but so too are seemingly straightforward and simple devices like page numbers, running heads, tables of contents, and indices. Considered "peritexts" – elements materially situated in relationship to the text – in Gerard Genette's formulation of the paratext, elements like tables of contents and indices are "the means by which a text makes a book of itself and proposes itself as such to its readers." Imbued with "illocutionary force," paratexts communicate.[270] We might also read peritexts such as the table of contents and index as maps that detail the topography of the text – its organization, contents, and topics as paths, nodes, and landmarks. These features act as corollaries to the material space of the bookstore, shaping and guiding reading and consumer practices and values.

American booksellers in the nineteenth and twentieth centuries experimented with how to organize book information through tables of contents and indices. Within American booksellers' catalogues, a table of contents or index might appear in the front or back of the catalogue or not at all. Booksellers might include a table of contents in one catalogue, but leave it out of the next. Or they might include both a contents list and an index. Usually presented in tabular format, these elements serve primarily as "navigational paratexts" to help locate places in the main text and facilitate forms of "non-linear, reference reading."[271] While their forms have not been stable across time or place, modern conventions dictate different logics of organization. The table of contents offers an account of the contents of a book by listing its divisions in sequential order, reflecting the architecture of the text.[272] The index, on the other hand, dissects the book's contents into individual topics or labels and organizes them alphabetically, rather than sequentially. The index, facilitated by the adoption of page numbers, is a "random-access technology."[273] Since the index abstracts and itemizes the text into non-sequential topics or labels, it is oriented toward the reader

[269] Drucker, "The Virtual Codex," para 26. [270] Genette, *Paratexts*, 6, 10.
[271] Howley, "Tables of Contents," 67, 71. [272] Nelson, "Table of Contents."
[273] Duncan, "Indexes," 265.

rather the text. The index reflects the reader's potential interests; the table of contents reflects the text's interests.[274]

The unique twentieth-century bookseller Loompanics, specializing in "the lunatic fringe of the libertarian movement," included both a table of contents organized by subject heading and a title index in their catalogues.[275] The contents pages in the 2003 Loompanics catalogue list self-defined subject headings sequentially, beginning with "Money-Making Opportunities" and "Underground Economy," then moving through such headings as "Revenge," "Head for the Hills," and "Reality Creation." Eschewing standard subject categories, this two-page unnumbered double-column list, which also includes a short description of the topic and page numbers, offers readers a reading of the bookstore, asserting not only their stock, but their philosophy as well. Over the next five pages, the catalogue also provides an index by book title. These multiple and consecutive structures of managing information offer different paths for reading and shopping, much as the bookstore offers individuals diverse means of moving through store space. The table of contents reflects a customer who navigates the bookstore according to desired subject headings or, in other words, according to the internal architecture of the bookstore – first to the biography section perhaps or to the "Revenge" section. The title index, on the other hand, empowers the reader by providing them a direct route to the desired book. Here is the bookstore shopper that values a targeted search among clearly organized stock. Not only structuring the reader's engagement with the catalogue text, the table of contents and index also reflect and encourage the spatialized consumer practices of the bookstore.

Akin to the shelving headings in the stores discussed in the second section, tables of contents also map epistemologies. The Loompanics subject headings offer specific areas of knowledge and ways of knowing according to its libertarian and anarchist philosophies. In another suggestive example, in the wake of the recent Black Lives Matter protests and racial justice activism, Bromer Booksellers released the print catalogue *Pressing Issues: Voices for Justice in the Book Arts* (2021), followed by an electronic

---

[274] Duncan, "Indexes," 265.   [275] Loompanics, *2003 The Best Book Catalog*.

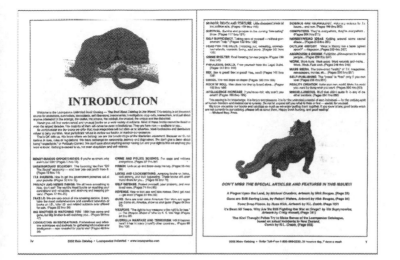

Figure 10 Loompanics, *2003 The Best Book Catalog* (2003). Image License: CC BY-NC-ND 3.0

version. The catalogue collects a diverse and international range of artistic texts focusing on social justice, identity, and equality and "aim[s] to elevate the voices of those who are too often silenced."[276] The items are organized into categories of social justice such as "Labor and Income Inequality," "Immigration," and "Black Lives"; these categories are listed in a sequential, color-coded table of contents. In addition, a "Coding Key" on the opposite page offers an additional navigation aid through twenty-six specific topics coded with an abbreviation. Examples include Ageism (AG), Drug Policy (DR), Education (ED), LGBTQ+ (++), Middle Eastern Lives (ME), and Public Health (PH). Each sale item in the catalogue includes all of its relevant codes on the side margin of each page. The table of contents and codes provide numerous paths for navigating the catalogue; one might delve into a specific category or skip around following

---

[276] *Pressing Issues*, iv. PDF edition available online.

Table of Contents

Coding Key

Ageism	AG
Anti-authoritarianism/government corruption	GC
Anti-colonialism	AC
Anti-consumerism	CC
Anti-militarism/Anti-war/Pacifism	AM
Anti-violence and gun control	AV
Black lives	BK
Censorship	CE
Disabilities and mental health	DM
Drug policy	DR
East Asian lives	EA
Education	ED
Environmental justice	EN
Foundational documents	FD
Immigration	IM
Indigenous lives	IN
Jewish lives	JE
Labor/income inequality	LI
Latinx lives	LX
LGBTQ+	++
Middle Eastern lives	ME
Police (miscarriages of justice)	PO
Protest	PR
Public health	PH
Women and gender	WG
Works on paper	・

Figure 11 "Table of Contents" and "Coding Key" in *Pressing Issues: Voices for Justice in the Book Arts* (2021). Credit: Bromer Booksellers & Gallery

a coded topic. As the reader physically navigates the catalogue, they conceptualize social justice, discerning its core concerns through subject categories and tracing the intersectional and compounding nature of oppression through codes. Similar to Hogan's "feminist shelf," discussed in Section 2, whereby physical adjacency of books on shelves help produce a critical vocabulary and connective threads for feminist inquiry, *Pressing Issues* uses its structuring elements to both shape and help readers navigate the epistemologies of social justice.[277]

In addition to shaping ways of knowing, the book catalogue can also participate in the bookstore's unique ability to craft community. Readers of themed bookselling catalogues share interests; those perusing *Pressing Issues* are incorporated into a community of booksellers interested and engaged in

---

[277] Hogan, *The Feminist Bookstore Movement*, 109.

social justice. The use of cover illustrations can create an imagined community of reader-consumers. In addition, the table of contents – and particularly, the "bookish" table of contents that includes prefatory and supplemental material beyond the book list – also contributes to this community-building work. In the 2003 Loompanics catalogue mentioned above, the two-page table of contents privileges the books for sale, but at the end of that content list, the catalogue reframes itself with both a quotation from its founder as well as a list of "Special articles and features" included in the catalogue: "This catalogue is for knowledge. It is for joy and pleasure."[278] The added articles, including illustrations and a comic as well as essays, invite readers to engage with the catalogue within a community of like-minded readers.

Likewise, a few nineteenth-century bookseller catalogues employed these bookish tables of contents. Putnam's 1861 *Classified Catalogue of Most Important Books* included a detailed table of contents at the front of the catalogue that lists a preface and sketch of the field of bibliography.[279] And Evans' & Co., mid-nineteenth-century New York and Philadelphia gift book enterprise booksellers, issued lengthy catalogues whose table of contents focused on the full catalogue rather than just the books for sale. Their 1858 New York catalogue not only included images of the exterior and interior of the store on front and back covers, it also included an "Index" on the title-page verso that blended sequential contents with an alphabetical subject list.[280] Beyond the book list, the contents include "To the public," an opening introduction to the store and its business model, "Inducements to Agents," "List of References," "Gift or Dividend System Explained," "The Poet and His Gift," a promotional poem advertising the store, and "Opinions of the Press." Blending the informational, the commercial, and the literary, this table of contents shapes the catalogue as a multifunctional genre for diverse reading and consumer audiences.

Evans' catalogue likewise offered a shared reading experience; its "to the public" addresses, solicitations of agents, and imaginative writing invite the

---

[278] Loompanics, *2003 The Best Book Catalog*.

[279] G. P. Putnam, *Classified Catalogue*.

[280] Evans & Co., *The Original Evans & Co.'s Great Gift Book Establishment*.

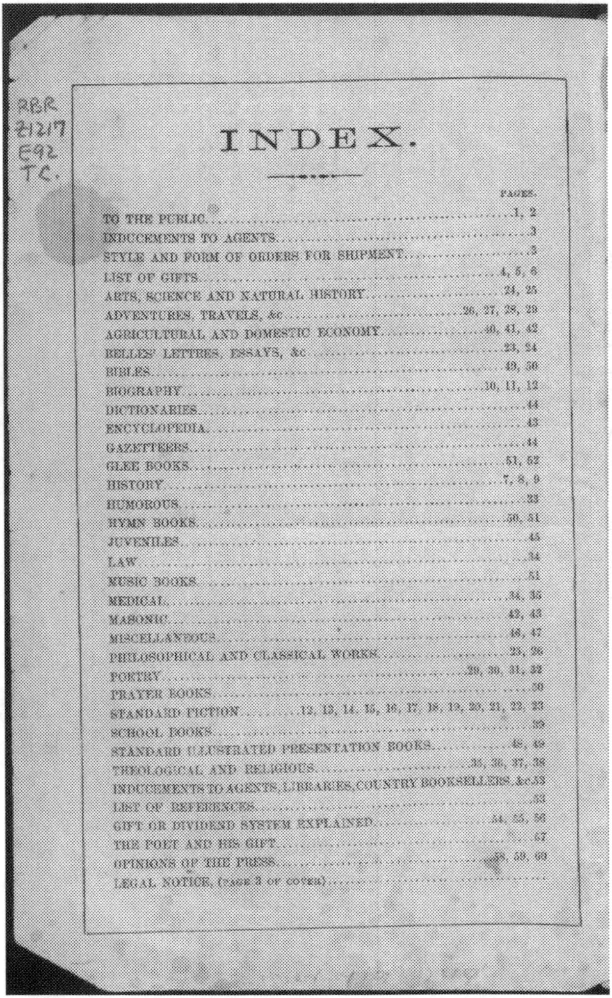

INDEX.

Figure 12 Evans & Co., *The Original Evans & Co.'s Great Gift Book Establishment* (New York, 1858). Courtesy, the Winterthur Library: Printed Book and Periodical Collection.

reader into the larger community of the bookstore and aim to consolidate a community of reader-customers that share in the bookstore's endeavor. In fact, this community functioned in physical space as well. Based on several surviving Evans catalogue order bills, we know that readers looked to their kinship and local proximity networks to create buying "clubs." Laura Deming, a stonemason's wife in 1859 Wethersfield, Connecticut, gathered her husband, next-door neighbor, and nearby families to submit a group order to Evans. G. R. Wells in DeKalb County, Georgia, included members of his family and professional connections in his order.[281] The pages of the catalogue invited these readers into the bookstore and both drew on and drew together community bonds.

4.5 Reflection

Considered as a wayfinding genre, bookseller catalogues seek not only to orient the reader in a bookselling space, but to actively create that space. By offering readers sites of interaction through such elements as covers, bookstore illustrations, and tables of contents and indices, they spatialize the bookstore, offering entry into an imagined social and consumer community and shaping practices and values of book buying and reading. Bookseller catalogues offer valuable evidence for diverse scholarly projects, but as texts in their own right, they deserve analysis of their structural and discursive composition and how these components work together to create meaning. Additional analysis might focus on a specific time period, geographic location, or individual bookseller or might take a closer look at other catalogue elements, like formats, item descriptions, or the use of illustration within the catalogue.

---

[281] Evans, D. W., *The Pioneer Gift Book Store*; Evans, G. G., *G.G. Evans' Original Gift Book Store*. See also Highland, "Gambling on a Sale."

5 Epilogue: Making Space

Bookselling today, like it has always been, is enmeshed in multiple spatial contexts. In Greensboro, North Carolina, BIPOC-owned Boomerang Bookshop: Nomad is a "book bus."[282] The light grey bus, with large doors, a pop-up back window, and pine bookcases, parks at area markets and traverses the roads of Central North Carolina. Featured by the Southern Independent Booksellers Alliance (SIBC), the Boomerang Bookshop is part of a recent expansion of membership eligibility to "stores with nontraditional and emerging bookstore models like pop-ups, bookmobiles, and book fairs."[283] The discussion to expand the bookselling spaces and forms recognized by SIBC was catalyzed in part by the disruptions of COVID. As the pandemic shifted our own spaces, refiguring material, interpersonal, and social boundaries, booksellers – like other retailers – creatively reorganized their book spaces. Bookshops moved outside under tents and onto tables, booksellers took to bikes for personal deliveries, and more and more independent booksellers adopted, or moved entirely to, digital bookselling.[284]

As the continued diversity and fluidity of modes of bookselling attests, we must look to and beyond the bookstore to understand the complex spatial and cultural geographies of bookselling. *Stores, Streets, and Pages* attempts to do this. While bookselling is often synonymous with bookstores, the less-studied aspects of contemporary street bookselling and the social and cultural work of bookselling catalogs deserve increased attention. The "Reflection" paragraphs in each section point to areas for further research in the specific spatial context of store, street, or page. In general, however, a greater understanding of the diversity of bookselling forms and spaces is needed. Many scholars, including those cited in this element, have

---

[282] Barber, "Boomerang brings back"; See also the store site: https://bookshop .org/shop/boomerangbookshop.

[283] "Come Together," para. 4; Rosen, "Another Pandemic Surprise: A Mini Indie Bookstore Boom," para. 9.

[284] Although digital spaces are outside of the scope of this element, online bookselling has its own spatial dynamics and dimensions, shaped in part though site aesthetics, functionality, and networks. Community may look different in online stores, but it is still present and actively crafted.

started and productively expanded this work, by examining feminist or Black book spaces, for instance. However, research on the history of bookselling is disproportionately focused on American and European contexts. Making space for more global approaches and attention to diverse communities would enrich our understanding of the unique and comparative ways booksellers and bookselling respond to and craft local spaces.

As the field of book history recognizes, bookselling is cultural work.[285] When we focus on the spaces of bookselling, we expose the variety of tensions embedded in this work – between commerce and idealism, between belonging and exclusion, and between regulation and innovation. We see how bookselling spaces – from the store to the street to the physical page – operate within insistently local social and commercial contexts and how these spaces can be used to create social community and to craft and consolidate individual identities and symbolic meaning. Bookselling will continue to assume new forms and engage in complex ways with sociospatial environments; understanding these dynamics is necessary for appreciating and advocating for the essential social work of bookselling and for ensuring resilient bookselling landscapes.

[285] Darnton, "What is the History of Books?" Darnton discusses booksellers as "cultural agents" (78).

Bibliography

Archival Sources

Appleton, D. & Co., *Catalogue of English Books in the several departments of literature. (Methodically arranged, with notes.) For sale by D. Appleton & Co., at their Literary Emporium, 200, Broadway, New-York. 1841* (New York: 1841). Collections of the American Antiquarian Society.

Appleton, D. & Co., *Catalogue of English Books, Modern Editions . . .. Theology and Divinity . . . Architecture and Engineering . . . Elegant Picturesque and Illustrated Works, Books of Print, Miscellaneous Books. Imported for Sale by D. Appleton & Co., at their European and American Bookstore* (New York, 1840). Collections of the American Antiquarian Society.

Appleton D. & Co., *Catalogue of an Extensive Collection of Rare and Valuable Old Books, recently imported from Europe: Comprising an assortment of Standard Works in Theological, Historical, Legal, and Miscellaneous Literature* (New York, 1835). Collections of the Grolier Club Library.

Baker & Taylor Co., *Bookselling*, Book Sales Promotion Bureau, The Baker & Taylor Co. In the *Rollo G. Silver: Files on American Printers and Publishers, ca. 1950*, Box 1, Baker & Taylor. Collections of the Grolier Club.

Book Supply Company, *Bargains in Books Illustrated Catalog*. Chicago: The Book Supply Co., 1933. Collections of the Grolier Club Library.

Burnham and Brothers, *Catalogue of Novels, Tales, Romances, Travels, Memoirs, Narratives, and other Miscellaneous Books*. Boston: Burnham & Brothers, 1850. Collections of the American Antiquarian Society.

Charles Scribner's Sons, First Editions of Famous American Songs. Catalogue No. 105. New York: The Scribner Book Store, [1936.] In collections of the Grolier Club Library.

Charles Scribner's Sons, First Editions of Juvenile Fiction 1814–1924. Catalogue No. 107. New York: The Scribner Book Store, 1936. Collections of the Grolier Club Library.

Doyle, John, *Part First. Catalogue of a Large and Valuable Collection of Ancient and Modern Books in Every Department of Human Knowledge; for Sale, at extremely Low Prices for Cash, by John Doyle, at the Cheap Ancient and Modern Bookstore, the Moral Centre of the Intellectual World, No. 146 Nassau Street, New York.* John Doyle: [May 1848]. Collections of the American Antiquarian Society.

Evans, D. W., *The Pioneer Gift Book Store. D.W. Evans & Co. 677 Broadway, New York. [Oct 20] 18[59] M[iss] Laura Deming.* New York, 1859. Ephemera Bill 0223. Collections of the American Antiquarian Society.

Evans, G. G., *G. G. Evans' Original Gift book store and Publishing house, no. 439 Chestnut Street, Philadelphia.* Collections of the Library Company of Philadelphia.

Evans & Co., *The Original Evans & Co.'s Great Gift Book Establishment* [catalogue]. New York, 1858, p. 2. Collections of Winterthur Library and Museum.

Gowans, William, *Gowans' Catalogue of American Books, for sale at the affixed prices, Store, 178 Fulton-St., New-York, Opposite St. Paul's Church-yard, a few doors west of Broadway* (New York, 1851). Collections of the Grolier Club Library.

"Interior View of Appleton's Book Store, 346 & 348 Broadway, New York," *The Historical Picture Gallery: or, Scenes and Incidents in American History* (Boston, 1856), The Miriam and Ira D. Wallach Division of Art, Prints and Photographs: Picture Collection, The

New York Public Library. https://digitalcollections.nypl.org/items/510d47e1-05 db-a3d9-e040-e00a18064a99.

"Leary's Old Bookstore," Philadelphia, 1893. Collections of The Library Company of Philadelphia.

Leggat Brothers, *Centennial Catalogue of a Fine Collection of English and American Books, all New and Fresh Stock, for Sale at the low prices affixed, by Leggat Brothers, No 3 Beekman Street (Bet. Nassau St. and City Hall Park), New York*. New York: Leggat Brothers, [1870]. Collections of the Grolier Club Library.

"Messrs. Lackington, Allen & Co., Temple of the Muses, Finsbury Square," Thomas H. Shepherd, 1828. Special Collections, Princeton University Library. https://library.princeton.edu/visual_materials/ga/temple%20of%20the%20muses.jpg

Prevost, Victor, D., "Appleton & Co., formerly N.Y. Library Building, Broadway between Leonard Street & Catharine Lane [200 Broadway]," Victor Prevost photograph collection, 1853–1857, undated. Collections of the New York Historical Society. https://digitalcollections.nyhistory.org/islandora/object/nyhs%3A74788

Putnam, G. P., *Classified Catalogue of the Most Important Books, in Nearly Every Department of Literature and Science: English and American Editions* (New York: G. P. Putman, 1861). Collections of the Grolier Club Library.

Reeve, T. W., *No. 8. A Descriptive and Priced Catalogue of a Collection of Valuable London Books, Just Imported From Europe*. New York: T. W. Reeve, November 17, 1857. Collections of the Grolier Club Library.

Reference List

"20–465 Restrictions on the placement of vehicles, pushcarts and stands; vending in certain areas prohibited," New York City Administrative Code, *American Legal Publishing Code Library*, https://codelibrary.amlegal.com/codes/newyorkcity/latest/NYCadmin/0-0-0-34251.

"About," *John Sandoe Books*, https://johnsandoe.com/about/.

Addis, Michela, "Understanding the Customer Journey to Create Excellent Customer Experiences in Bookshops," *International Journal of Marketing Studies* 8: 4 (2016), 20–36, https://doi.org/10.5539/ijms.v8n4p20.

Anjaria, Jonathan Shapiro, "Street Hawkers and Public Space in Mumbai," *Economic and Political Weekly* 41: 21 (2006), 2140–2146. https://doi.org/10.2307/4418270.

Antonsich, Marco, "Searching for Belonging – An Analytical Framework," *Geography Compass* 4: 6 (June 2010), 644–659. https://doi.org/10.1111/j.1749-8198.2009.00317.x.

"Appleton's New Head-quarters," *Christian Advocate* (March 16, 1871), 83. *American Periodicals Series*.

Arango, Tim, "Syrian Migrants in Istanbul Confront Choice: Stay or Move On," *The New York Times* (December 25, 2015). www.nytimes.com/2015/12/24/world/europe/syrian-migrants-in-istanbul-confront-choice-stay-or-move-on.html.

Ariail, Kate Dobbs, "Durham's Book Exchange Closes Its Doors," *Indy Week* (February 11, 2009). https://indyweek.com/culture/art/durhams-book-exchange-closes-doors/.

Atkinson, David and Steve Roud, *Street Literature of the Long Nineteenth Century: Producers, Sellers, Consumers* (Newcastle upon Tyne: Cambridge Scholars, 2017).

Augst, Thomas and Kenneth Carpenter (eds.), *Institutions of Reading: The Social Life of Libraries in the United States* (Amherst: University of Massachusetts Press, 2007).

Bachelard, Gaston, *The Poetics of Space* (Boston: Beacon Press, 1994).

Barber, Lauren, "Boomerang Brings Back the Book Bus," *Triad City Beat* (May 31, 2017), https://triad-city-beat.com/boomerang-bookshop-brings-back-book-bus/.

Barnes, Alison, "Geo/Graphic Design: The Liminal Space of the Page," *Geographical Review* 103: 2 (April 2013), 164–176. https://doi.org/10.1111/gere.12006.

Beale, Nigel, "Don Lindgren on the Importance of Bookseller Catalogues," *The Biblio File*, July 3, 2021, Podcast, https://thebibliofile.ca/don-lindgren-on-the-importance-of-bookseller-catalogues.

Bergmann, Joy, "NYPD Again Confiscates Controversial Sidewalk Bookseller's Inventory," *West Side Rag* (August 3, 2018), www.westsiderag.com/2018/08/03/nypd-again-confiscates-controversial-sidewalk-booksellers-inventory.

Black, Fiona A., Jennifer M. Grek Martin, and Bertrum H. MacDonald, "Geographic Information Systems and Book History," in *Oxford Research Encyclopedia, Literature* (Oxford: Oxford University Press, 2021), https://doi.org/10.1093/acrefore/9780190201098.013.1151.

Blain, Keisha N., "Community Politics and Grassroots Activism during the 1920s: An Interview with Shannon King," *AAIHS*. Blog (December 10, 2015). www.aaihs.org/community-politics/.

Bluestone, Daniel M., "'The Pushcart Evil': Peddlers, Merchants, and New York City's Streets, 1890-1940," *Journal of Urban History* 18: 1 (November 1991), 68–92.

Boehm, Matt, "Peddler Poets: Itinerant Print Dissemination and Literary Access in Antebellum America," *The Journal of the Midwest Modern Language Association* 42: 1 (2009): 1–14.

Young, D. W., *The Booksellers* [film] (Blackletter Films, 2020), https://booksellersdocumentary.com/.

Bridges, William and Peter Maverick, *This map of the city of New York and island of Manhattan, as laid out by the commissioners appointed by the legislature, April 3d,is respectfully dedicated to the mayor, aldermen and commonalty thereof* (New York: s.n, 1811), Map. www.loc.gov/item/2005625335/.

Campbell, Lisa, "Foyles' New Flagship Opens Its Doors," *The Bookseller* (June 5, 2014). www.thebookseller.com/news/foyles-new-flagship-opens-its-doors.

Carr, Jane Greenway, "We Must Seek on the Highways the Unconverted': Kathryn Magnolia Johnson and Literary Activism on the Road," *American Quarterly* 67: 2 (2015), 443–470. https://doi.org/10.1353/aq.2015.0020.

Carrión, Jorge, *Bookshops: A Reader's History*, Trans. Peter Bush (Windsor, Ontario: Biblioasis, 2017).

Chartier, Roger, *The Order of Books: Readers, Authors, and Libraries in Europe between the Fourteenth and Eighteenth Centuries* (Redwood City, CA: Stanford University Press, 1992).

Cohen, Anouk, "The Distribution of Knowledge and the Material Presence of Books: The Sidewalk Book Vendors of Rabat and Casablanca, Morocco," trans. John Angell, *Ethnologie Française* 165: 1 (2017), 23–36.

Cohen, Joanna, *Luxurious Citizens: The Politics of Consumption in Nineteenth-Century America* (Philadelphia: University of Pennsylvania Press, 2017).

"Come Together! The Magical Mystery Bookstore, News you can use from the Land of SIBA March 3, 2022," Newsletter, *Southern Independent Booksellers Alliance* (March 3, 2022), https://sibaweb.com/page/siba land_20220303?&hhsearchterms=%22bookmobile%22.

Connor, Jackson, "Brooklyn's Nkiru Books Rises Up Once More With Help From Talib Kweli," *Village Voice* (January 26, 2016). www.villagevoice.com/2016/01/26/brooklyns-nkiru-books-rises-up-once-more-with-help-from-talib-kweli/.

Coppens, Christian and Angela Nuovo, "Printed catalogues of booksellers as a source for the history of the book trade," in Giovanna Granata and Angela Nuovo (eds.), *Selling and Collecting: Printed Book Sale Catalogues and Private Libraries in Early Modern Europe* (Macerata: eum, 2018), 145–160.

Cresswell, Tim, *On the Move: Mobility in the Modern Western World* (New York: Routledge, 2006).

Darnton, Robert, "What is the History of Books," *Daedalus* 111: 3 (Summer 1982), 65–83, www.jstor.org/stable/20024803#metadata_info_tab_contents.

Davis, Joshua Clark, "The FBI's War on Black-Owned Bookstores," *The Atlantic* (February 19, 2018). www.theatlantic.com/politics/archive/2018/02/fbi-black-bookstores/553598/.

Davis, Joshua Clark, *From Head Shops to Whole Foods: The Rise and Fall of Activist Entrepreneurs* (New York: Columbia University Press, 2017). https://doi.org/10.7312/davi17158.

de Certeau, Michel, *The Practice of Everyday Life*. Trans. Steven Rendall (Berkeley: University of California Press, 1984).

Delap, Lucy, "Feminist Bookshops, Reading Cultures and the Women's Liberation Movement in Great Britain, c. 1974–2000," *History Workshop Journal* 81: 1 (April 1, 2016), 171–196, https://doi.org/10.1093/hwj/dbw002.

Derricotte, Toi, "Bookstore," *I: New and Selected Poems* (Pittsburgh: University of Pittsburgh Press, 2019), 188.

der Weduwen, Arthur, Pettegree Andrew and Kent Graeme, *Book Trade Catalogues in Early Modern Europe* (Leiden, The Netherlands: Brill, 2021).

Devlin, Ryan Thomas, "Street Vending and the Politics of Space in New York City," in Kristina Graaff and Noa Ha (eds.), *Street Vending in the Neoliberal City: A Global Perspective on the Practices and Policies of a Marginalized Economy* (New York: Berghahn Books, 2015), 43–58.

"Do We Want Kiosks?" *The Newsman: A Journal for Newsdealers, Publishers, Booksellers, and Kindred Trades* 8: 2(New York, February 1891), 2.

Drucker, Johanna, "The Virtual Codex from Page Space to E-space," in Susan Schreibman and Ray Siemens (eds.), *A Companion to Digital*

Literary Studies (Oxford: Blackwell, 2008). www.digitalhumanities.org /companionDLS/.

Dumond, Annie Nelles, *Annie Nelles, or, The Life of a Book Agent: An Autobiography*, Life of a Book Agent (Cincinnati: A. Nelles, 1868), https://catalog.hathitrust.org/Record/003456805.

Duncan, Dennis, "Indexes" in Dennis Duncan and Ada, Smyth (eds.), *Book Parts* (Oxford: Oxford University Press, 2019), 263–274.

Duneier, Mitchell, *Sidewalk* (New York: Farrar, Straus and Giroux, 2001).

Edwards, Steve, "On the Experience of Entering a Bookstore in Your Forties (vs. Your Twenties)," *Literary Hub* (January 3, 2019). https:// lithub.com/on-the-experience-of-entering-a-bookstore-in-your-forties-vs-your-twenties/.

Emblidge, David M., "City Lights Bookstore: 'A Finger in the Dike,'" *Publishing Research Quarterly* 21: 4 (2005): 30–39. https://doi.org/10 .1007/s12109-005-0030-9.

Emerson, Ralph Waldo, "Self-Reliance," in Joel Porte (ed.), *Emerson: Essays and Lectures* (New York: The Library of America, 1983), 257–282.

Fein, Esther B., "The Media Business; Bookstores' Growing Rival: Bargains on the Curb," *New York Times* (October 5, 1992). www .nytimes.com/1992/10/05/business/the-media-business-bookstores-growing-rival-bargains-on-the-curb.html.

Fama, Ben, "Interview with a Bookseller: Ben Fama with Vortexity Books' Jen Fisher," *Newest York* (n.d), www.newestyork.co/jen-fisher.

Franz, Kathleen, "The Open Road: Automobility and Racial Uplift in the Interwar Years," in Bruce Sinclair (ed.), *Technology and the African-American Experience: Needs and Opportunities for Study* (Cambridge: MIT Press, 2004), 131–153.

Fredgant, Don, *American Trade Catalogs* (Paducah, KY: Collector Books, 1984).

Ganser, Alexandra, *Roads of Her Own: Gendered Space and Mobility in American Women's Road Narratives, 1970–2000* (Amsterdam: Rodopi, 2009).

Garcia, John J., "The 'Curiousaffaire' of Mason Locke Weems: Nationalism, the Book Trade, and Printed Lives in the Early United States," *The Papers of the Bibliographical Society of America* 108: 4 (2014), 453–475, https://doi.org/10.1086/681567.

"Gem in the Dirt, Sunday Open Book Bazaar at Anarkali Lahore," *Locally Lahore* (April 14, 2017), www.locallylahore.com/jem-dirt-sunday-open-book-bazaar-anarkali-lahore/.

Genette, Gérard, *Paratexts: Thresholds of Interpretation*, Jane E. Lewin, trans. (Cambridge: Cambridge University Press, 1997).

Golledge, Reginald, *Wayfinding Behavior: Cognitive Mapping and Other Spatial Processes* (Baltimore: Johns Hopkins University Press, 1999).

Graaff, Kristina, "Ethnic Contestations over African American Fiction: The Street Vending of Street Literature in New York City," in Kristina Graaff and Noa Ha (eds.), *Street Vending in the Neoliberal City: A Global Perspective on the Practices and Policies of a Marginalized Economy* (New York: Berghahn Books, 2015), 117–135.

Graaff, Kristina and Noa Ha, "Introduction. Street Vending in the Neoliberal City: A Global Perspective on the Practices and Policies of a Marginalized Economy," in Kristina Graaff and Noa Ha (eds.), *Street Vending in the Neoliberal City: A Global Perspective on the Practices and Policies of a Marginalized Economy* (New York: Berghahn Books, 2015), 1–17.

Green, Victor Hugo, *The Negro motorist Green-book* (New York City: V.H. Green, 1936), www.loc.gov/item/2016298176/.

Greene, Lorenzo J., *Selling Black History for Carter G. Woodson: A Diary, 1930–1933*, Ed. Arvarh E. Strickland (Columbia: University of Missouri Press, 2018).

Griffiths, Alyn, "Colour-coded Books Produce a Rainbow-like Display in a Rio Bookshop by Studio Arthur Casas," *dezeen* (September 27, 2014). www.dezeen.com/2014/09/27/saraiva-bookstore-studio-arthur-casas/.

Grimstad, Kirsten and Susan Rennie, *The New Woman's Survival Catalog* (New York: Coward, McCann & Geoghegan, 1973).

Growoll, Adolph, *Book-Trade Bibliography in the United States in the Nineteenth Century* (1898; Reprint, New York: Burt Franklin, 1939).

Hackenberg, Michael, "The Subscription Publishing Network in Nineteenth-Century America," in Michael Hackenberg (ed.), *Getting the Books Out: Papers of the Chicago Conference on the Book in 19th-Century America* (Honolulu, HI: University Press of the Pacific, 2005), 45–75.

Hamilton, Mae, "Casa de Resistancia Bookstore Serves as a Refuge for UT Students," *The Daily Texan* (June 25, 2016). https://thedailytexan.com/2016/06/25/casa-de-resistencia-bookstore-serves-as-refuge-for-ut-students/.

Hellinga, Lotte, "Sale Advertisements for Books Printed in the Fifteenth Century," in Robin Myers, Michael Harris, and Giles Mandebrote (eds.), *Books for Sale: The Advertising and Promotion of Print since the Fifteenth Century* (Wilmington, DE: Oak Knoll Press, 2009), 1–26.

Henkin, David M., *City Reading: Written Words and Public Spaces In Antebellum New York* (New York: Columbia University Press, 1998).

Henley, Jon, "Through Gilets Jaunes, Strikes and Covid, Paris's 400-Year-Old Book Stalls Fight to Survive," *The Guardian* (December 29, 2020), www.theguardian.com/world/2020/dec/29/gilets-jaunes-strikes-and-covid-paris-bouquinistes-book-stalls-fight-for-survival.

Highland, Kristen Doyle. "Gambling on a Sale: Gift-Enterprise Bookselling and Communities of Print in 1850s America," *Knygotyra* 78 (2022), 17–45. https://doi.org/10.15388/Knygotyra.2022.78.105.

Highland, Kristen Doyle, "In the Bookstore: The Houses of Appleton and Book Cultures in Antebellum New York City," *Book History* 19 (2016), 214–255. https://doi.org/10.1353/bh.2016.0006.

Hilderbrand, Elin, "Nantucket Bookworks, Nantucket, Massachusetts," in Ronald Rice and Booksellers Across North America (eds.), *My Bookstore: Writers Celebrate Their Favorite Places to Browse, Read, and Shop* (New York: Black Dog & Leventhal, 2017), 152–155.

Hill, Marc Lamont, Biany Perez, and Decoteau J. Irby, "Street Fiction: What Is It and What Does It Mean for English Teachers?" *The English Journal* 97: 3 (January 2008), 76–81, https://doi.org/10.2307/30046836.

Hogan, Kristen, *The Feminist Bookstore Movement: Lesbian Antiracism and Feminist Accountability* (Durham: Duke University Press, 2016).

Hooks, Adam G., "Booksellers' Catalogues and the Classification of Printed Drama in Seventeenth-century England," *The Papers of the Bibliographical Society of America*, 102: 4 (December 2008), 445–464.

hooks, bell, *Art on My Mind: Visual Politics* (New York: New Press, 1995).

hooks, bell, *Yearning: Race. Gender, and Cultural Politics* (Boston: South End Press, 1990).

Howard, Brian Clark, "This is the World's Most Beautiful Bookstore," *National Geographic* (January 4, 2019). www.nationalgeographic.com/travel/article/things-to-see-beautiful-bookshop.

Howitt, Chad, *Welcome to The Last Bookstore: A Short Documentary*, Online film (2016), www.lastbookstorela.com/about.

Howley, Joseph A., "Tables of Contents," in Dennis Duncan and Ada, Smyth (eds.), *Book Parts* (Oxford: Oxford University Press, 2019), 65–80.

Hruschka, John, *How Books Came to America: The Rise of the American Book Trade* (University Park, PA: Penn State University Press, 2012).

Jacobs, Jane, *The Death and Life of American Cities* (New York: Vintage Books, 2016 [1961]).

Jaffee, David, "Peddlers of Progress and the Transformation of the Rural North, 1760–1860," *The Journal of American History* 78: 2 (September 1991), 511–535.

Jennings, Angel, "Eso Won Books: Where the Black Experience is Chronicled and Cultivated," *Los Angeles Times* (February 26, 2018), www.latimes.com/local/california/la-me-eso-won-books-20160225-story.html.

Johns, Adrian, *The Nature of the Book: Print and Knowledge in the Making* (Chicago: University of Chicago Press, 1998).

Jones, Claire L., "Instruments of Medical Information: The Rise of the Medical Trade Catalog in Britain, 1750–1914," *Technology and Culture* 54: 3 (July 2013), 563–599. https://doi.org/10.1353/tech.2013.0114.

Kilgannon, Corey, "A Sidewalk Vendor Amasses Books, Summonses and Lawsuits," *New York Times* (August 10, 2016), www.nytimes.com/2016/08/11/nyregion/a-sidewalk-vendor-amasses-books-summonses-and-law suits.html.

Kim, Annette M., "The Mixed-Use Sidewalk," *Journal of the American Planning Association* 78: 3 (July 1, 2012): 225–238, https://doi.org/10.1080/01944363.2012.715504.

Kinder, Kimberley, *The Radical Bookstore: Counterspace for Social Movements* (Minneapolis: University of Minnesota Press, 2021). https://doi.org/10.5749/j.ctv1h7zn3f.1.

Klanten, Robert and Lucas Feireiss (eds.), *Build-On: Converted Architecture and Transformed Buildings* (Berlin: Gestalten, 2009).

Kravitz, Melissa, "Sisters Uptown Bookstore Celebrating Black culture in Harlem for Nearly 20 Years," *AMNY* (February 19, 2019). www.amny.com/things-to-do/sisters-uptown-bookstore-1-27446204/.

Kwisnek, Kristen, "Get an In-Depth Look At a Barnes & Noble Concept Store," *Book Riot* (May 19, 2019). https://bookriot.com/barnes-and-noble-concept-store/.

Langegger, Sig, *Rights to Public Space: Law, Culture, and Gentrification in the American West* (Cham, Switzerland: Palgrave Macmillan, 2017), https://doi.org/10.1007/978-3-319-41177-4_6.

Lefebvre, Henri, *The Production of Space* (Hoboken, NJ: Wiley-Blackwell, 1992).

Lindgren, Don, "Don Lindgren on the Importance of Bookseller Catalogues." Podcast. *The Bibliofile, Hosted by Nigel Beale.* https://thebibliofile.ca/don-lindgren-on-the-importance-of-bookseller-catalogues.

Liu, Ya-Ting, "A Right To Vend: New Policy Framework for Fostering Street Based Entrepreneurs in New York City," unpublished Ph.D. thesis, Massachusetts Institute of Technology (2007).

Loesch, Sheila, "Why Working in a Bookstore was so Disappointing." *Book Riot* (January 27, 2020). https://bookriot.com/working-in-a-book store-was-disappointing/.

Loompanics, *2003 The Best Book Catalog in the World* (Port Townsend: Loompanics Unlimited, 2003). Available via Internet Archive: https://archive.org/details/Loompanics_Catalog_2003/.

Loukaitou-Sideris, Anastasia, Renia Ehrenfeucht, and Robert Gottlieb, *Sidewalks: Conflict and Negotiation over Public Space* (Cambridge: MIT Press, 2009), http://ebookcentral.proquest.com/lib/aus-ebooks/detail.action?docID=3339011.

Lu, Yi and Hyun-Bo Seo, "Developing Visibility Analysis for a Retail Store: A Pilot Study in a Bookstore," *Environment and Planning B: Planning and Design* 42 (2015), 95–109. https://doi.org/10.1068/b130016p.

Lynch, Kevin, *The Image of the City* (Cambridge: MIT Press, 1960).

Maclean, Ian, "Book Sales Catalogs," in Ann Blair, Paul Duguid, Anja-Silvia Goeing, and Anthony Grafton (eds.), *Information: A Historical Companion* (Princeton: Princeton University Press, 2021), 339–342.

Malkin, Peter L, "Book Vendors Shouldn't Have Any Sidewalk Privileges," letter to the Editor. *New York Times* (October 19, 1992), www.nytimes.com/1992/10/19/opinion/l-book-vendors-shouldn-t-have-any-sidewalk-privileges-985392.html.

Massey, Doreen, *Space, Place, and Gender* (Minneapolis: University of Minnesota Press, 1994.

Mather, Cotton, "11 d. 4 m," in Worthington Chauncey Ford (ed.), *Diary of Cotton Mather, Volume I, 1681–1708* (Boston: Massachusetts Historical Society, 1708), 65.

Mattern, Shannon, "Fugitive Libraries," *Places Journal* (October 2019), https://doi.org/10.22269/191022.

McHenry, Elizabeth, *Forgotten Readers: Recovering the Lost History of African American Literary Societies.* (Durham: Duke University Press, 2002).

McHenry, Elizabeth, "Reading and Race Pride: The Literary Activism of Black Clubwomen," in Carl F. Kaestle and Janice A. Radway (eds.), *A History of the Book in America : Volume 4: Print in Motion: the Expansion of Publishing and Reading in the United States, 1880–1940* (Chapel Hill: University of North Carolina Press, 2009), 491–510.

Mee, Kathleen and Sarah Wright, "Geographies of Belonging," *Environment and Planning A: Economy and Space* 41: 4 (April 1, 2009): 772–779, https://doi.org/10.1068/a41364.

Miller, Laura J., *Reluctant Capitalists: Bookselling and the Culture of Consumption* (Chicago: Chicago University Press, 2006).

Morris, Ali, "LUO Studio Uses Rotating Walls to Create Flexible Beijing Bookshop," *dezeen* (June 20, 2021), www.dezeen.com/2021/06/20/mumokuteki-luo-studio-beijing-bookstore-interior/.

Murphy, James L., "The 'Unbelievable' Odyssey of Annie Nelles Dumond; A Minor Literary Mystery Solved," *Ohio Genealogical Society Quarterly* 50: 4 (Summer 2010), 179–186.

Muse, Eben J., *Fantasies of the Bookstore*. Elements in Publishing and Book Culture (Cambridge: Cambridge University Press, 2022).

Nadelson, Reggie, "In Greenwich Village, the Perfect New York Bookstore Lives On," *The New York Times, T Magazine* (November 25, 2019). www.nytimes.com/2019/11/25/t-magazine/three-lives-bookstore.html.

Naison, Mark, "Street Vending, Political Activism, and Community Building in African American History: The Case of Harlem," in Kristina Graaff and Noa Ha (eds.), *Street Vending in the Neoliberal City: A Global Perspective on the Practices and Policies of a Marginalized Economy* (New York: Berghahn Books, 2015), 219–232.

Nelson, Brent, "Table of Contents," in Yin Liu (ed.), *ArchBook: Architectures of the Book*, (Saskatoon, SK: University of Saskatchewan, 2022) , https://drc.usask.ca/projects/archbook/entries.php.

Nelson, Vaunda Micheaux, *No Crystal Star: A Documentary Novel of the Life and Work of Lewis Michaux* (Minneapolis, MN: Carolrhoda Lab, 2013).

New York City Police Department, *The Peddler Handbook*, National Institute of Justice, NCJ Number 145611 (New York, 1991), www.ojp.gov/ncjrs/virtual-library/abstracts/peddler-handbook.

Nord, David Paul, *Faith in Reading: Religious Publishing and the Birth of Mass Media in America* (Oxford: Oxford University Press, 2004).

Ogborn, Miles and Charles W. J. Withers, *Geographies of the Book* (Surrey: Ashgate, 2010).

Oldenburg, Ramon and Dennis Brissett, "The Third Place," *Qualitative Sociology* 5: 4 (December 1, 1982): 265–284, https://doi.org/10.1007/BF00986754.

Osborne, Huw, "Introduction: Openings," in Huw Osborne, Ann R. Hawkins, and Maura Ives (eds.), *The Rise of the Modernist Bookshop: Books and the Commerce of Culture in the Twentieth Century* (London: Taylor & Francis, 2015), 1–14.

Ovington, Mary White, "Selling Race Pride," *The Publishers Weekly the American Book Trade Journal*, 107: 2 (January 10, 1925): 111–114.

Smith, Ed, "PBO Noir Expert Kurt Brokaw Live on the Streets of NYC," video posted by Ed Smith (December 21, 2016), www.youtube.com/watch?v=jYC9anWIeXQ.

Pages, *Pages Bookstore Café Istanbul*, May 15, 2021, http://pagesbookstorecafe.com/istanbul/.

Paterson, Mark, *Consumption and Everyday Life* (London: Routledge, 2006).

Payne, John R., *Great Catalogues by Master Booksellers: A Selection of American and English Booksellers' Catalogues, 19th-21st Century* (Austin, TX: Roger Beacham, 2017).

Street Vendor Project, *Peddling Uphill: A Report on the Condition of Street Vendors in New York City*, A Report by the Street Vendor Project of the Urban Justice Center (New York, 2006), http://streetvendor.org/publications/.

Petroski, Henry, *The Book on the Bookshelf* (New York: Alfred A. Knopf, 1999).

Bromer Booksellers, *Pressing Issues: Voices for Justice in the Book Arts* (Boston, MA: Bromer Booksellers, 2021), www.bromer.com/catalogues.php. PDF: www.bromer.com/images/upload/socialjusticecat-web.pdf.

Pollard, Graham and Ehrman Albert, *The Distribution of Books by Catalogue from the Invention of Printing to A.D. 1800, Based on Material in the Broxbourne Library* (Cambridge: Printed for presentation to members of the Roxburghe Club, 1965).

"Pushcart Wars," *Gotham Gazette* (n.d.), www.gothamgazette.com/index.php/superman/2366-pushcart-wars.

Ratkovic, Milan, *La légend des Bouquinistes de Paris* (Lausanne:L'âge d'homme, 2006).

Raven, James, *Bookscape: Geographies of Printing and Publishing in London before 1800* (London: The British Library, 2014).

Raven, James, *The Business of Books: Booksellers and the English Book Trade, 1450–1850* (New Haven: Yale University Press, 2011).

Raven, James and Leslie Howsam (eds.), *Books between Europe and the Americas: Connections and Communities, 1620–1860* (London: Palgrave Macmillan, 2011).

"The Regulation of Street Vendors" *NYCLU* (May 4, 2005), www.nyclu.org/en/publications/regulation-street-vendors.

Rosen, Judith, "Another Pandemic Surprise: A Mini Indie Bookstore Boom," *Publisher's Weekly* (October 15, 2021), www.publishersweekly.com/pw/by-topic/industry-news/bookselling/article/87648-another-pandemic-surprise-a-mini-indie-bookstore-boom.html.

SA Booksellers Association, *Bookshop Marketing*, https://lms.tuit.co.za/courses/219/pages/place?module_item_id=12612.

Scharff, Virginia, *Taking the Wheel: Women and the Coming of the Motor Age* (New York: Free Press, 1991).

Seager, Joni, "International Women," *Feminist Bookstore News* 11: 3 (September 1, 1988), 42–44, www.jstor.org/stable/community.28036322.

Seiler, Cotton, *Republic of Drivers: A Cultural History of Automobility in America* (Chicago: University of Chicago Press, 2009).

Sennett, Richard, *The Fall of Public Man: On the Social Psychology of Capitalism* (New York: Vintage Books, 1978).

Shaheen, Kareem, "Istanbul Bookshop that Transports Young Syrians Back Home," *The Guardian* (January 23, 2017). www.theguardian.com/world/2017/jan/23/istanbul-bookshop-that-transports-young-syrians-back-home.

Smith, Steven Carl, "Space," *Early American Studies: An Interdisciplinary Journal* 16: 4 (2018), 764–776, https://doi.org/10.1353/eam.2018.0047.

Soja, Edward W., *Thirdspace: Journeys to Los Angeles and Other Real-and-Imagined Places* (Cambridge, MA: Blackwell, 1996).

Solof, Mark, 'Let's Look Closer at Sidewalk Bookselling,' letter to the Editor, *New York Times* (November 9, 1992), www.nytimes.com/1992/11/09/opinion/l-let-s-look-closer-at-sidewalk-bookselling-560392.html.

Stern, Madeleine B., "Dissemination of Popular Books in the Midwest and Far West during the Nineteenth Century," in Michael Hackenberg (ed.), *Getting the Books Out: Papers of the Chicago Conference on the Book in 19ᵗʰ-Century America* (Honolulu, HI: University Press of the Pacific, 2005), 76–97.

NYC Business Solutions, "Street Vending," *New York City Government Educational Sector Guides* (n.d.), www.nyc.gov/html/sbs/nycbiz/downloads/pdf/educational/sector_guides/street_vending.pdf.

Strong, George Templeton, "Nov 3, 1836," in Allan Nevins and Milton Halsey Thomas (eds.), *The Diary of George Templeton Strong, 1835–1875*, Vol. 1 (New York: Octagon Books, 1952), 41.

"Successful Bookselling, Newburgh's Ingenious Bookseller," *Publisher's Weekly* 94: 2 (July 13, 1918), 12–13.

Tattered Cover Book Store, "Tattered History," (March 12, 2011). www.tatteredcover.com/tattered-history.

Taylor, Archer, *Book Catalogues: Their Varieties and Uses* (Chicago: Newberry Library, 1957).

The Street Vendor Project, "FAQ." *http://streetvendor.org/faq/*.

Fatima, Mahnoor, "Lahore's Sunday Book Bazaar," *Youlin Magazine* (December 9, 2019), www.youlinmagazine.com/article/lahore-sunday-book-bazaar/MTYyNA.

Tuan, Yi-Fu, *Topophilia: A Study of Environmental Perception, Attitudes and Values* (1974. Reprint New York: Columbia University Press, 1990).

Underhill, Paco, *Why We Buy: The Science of Shopping* (New York: Simon & Schuster, 2009).

Upton, Dell, *Another City: Urban Life and Urban Spaces in the New American Republic* (New Haven: Yale University Press, 2008).

Van Slyck, Abigail A., *Free to All: Carnegie Libraries and American Culture, 1890–1920* (Chicago: University of Chicago Press, 1995).

von la Valette, Desirée (ed.), *Cool Shops New York* (Kempen, Germany: teNeues, 2005).

Waite, Diana S., *The Architecture of Downtown Troy: An Illustrated History* (Albany: State University of New York Press, 2019).

Warner, Susan [Elizabeth Wetherell], *The Wide, Wide World* (New York: G.P. Putnam & Company, 1854).

West, James L. W., *American Authors and the Literary Marketplace since 1900* (Philadelphia: University of Pennsylvania Press, 1988).

Winans, Robert B., *A Descriptive Checklist of Book Catalogues Separately Printed in America, 1693–1800* (Worcester: American Antiquarian Society, 1981).

Wolfe, Gerald R., *The House of Appleton* (Metuchen, NJ: The Scarecrow Press, 1981).

Zboray, Ronald J., *A Fictive People: Antebellum Economic Development and the American Reading Public* (New York: Oxford University Press, 1993).

Zboray, Ronald J. and Mary Saracino Zboray, "The Boston Booktrades, 1789–1850: A Statistical and Geographical Analysis," in Conrad Edick Wright and Katheryn P. Viens (eds.), *Entrepreneurs: The Boston Business Community, 1750–1850* (Boston: Northeastern University Press, 1997), 210–67.

Zboray, Ronald J. and Mary Saracino Zboray, *Literary Dollars and Social Sense: A People's History of the Mass Market Book* (New York: Routledge, 2005).

Acknowledgments

I owe a debt of gratitude to many individuals and institutions for their support throughout this project.

Samantha Raynor and Eben Muse as series editors, as well as the team at Cambridge University Press have provided guidance and encouragement throughout the project. Samantha and Eben have also gifted me their extraordinary patience in the wake of the challenges of COVID-19. I am also grateful to the anonymous reviewers for their positive feedback and constructive suggestions. Any shortcomings of the minigraph are entirely my own.

The research on myriad book spaces has been a project of many years, in many different forms. I am grateful to the archival institutions that have provided fellowship opportunities, including the Library Company of Philadelphia's William Reese Company Fellowship, the American Antiquarian Society's Stephen Botein Fellowship, and the Grolier Club Library's William H. Helfand Fellowship. I have also haunted the archives of the Winterthur Library, Hagley Library, Temple University Library Special Collections, and others, and in all of these libraries over the years I have benefited from the generosity and expertise of its librarians, archivists, and other extraordinary staff. These individuals include Jim Green, Connie King, Emily Guthrie, Kathy Coyle, Paul Erickson, Ashley Cataldo, Meghan Constantinou, and Scott Ellwood. In addition to the fellowships mentioned above, American University of Sharjah also supported the writing of the manuscript with a faculty research grant.

Community is one of the keywords of this element, and certainly, writing takes a community. I am lucky to live in a wonderful community of colleagues and friends-as-family at the American University of Sharjah who provide the intellectual stimulation and the laughs that are needed to keep going. My kids will probably be disappointed that this is "the book" I've been working on (and not a guide to Roblox), but they've shown up with snacks and entertaining musings throughout. And Ryan Highland has devoted as much time to this project as I have in immeasurably supportive ways.

Cambridge Elements ≡

Publishing and Book Culture

SERIES EDITOR
Samantha Rayner
University College London

Samantha Rayner is Professor of Publishing and Book Cultures
at UCL. She is also Director of UCL's Centre for Publishing,
co-Director of the Bloomsbury CHAPTER (Communication
History, Authorship, Publishing, Textual Editing and
Reading) and co-Chair of the Bookselling Research Network.

ASSOCIATE EDITOR
Leah Tether
University of Bristol

Leah Tether is Professor of Medieval Literature and Publishing
at the University of Bristol. With an academic background in
medieval French and English literature and a professional
background in trade publishing, Leah has combined her
expertise and developed an international research profile in
book and publishing history from manuscript to digital.

ABOUT THE SERIES

This series aims to fill the demand for easily accessible, quality texts available for teaching and research in the diverse and dynamic fields of Publishing and Book Culture. Rigorously researched and peer-reviewed Elements will be published under themes, or 'Gatherings'. These Elements should be the first check point for researchers or students working on that area of publishing and book trade history and practice: we hope that, situated so logically at Cambridge University Press, where academic publishing in the UK began, it will develop to create an unrivalled space where these histories and practices can be investigated and preserved.

Cambridge Elements ≡

Publishing and Book Culture

Bookshops and Bookselling

Gathering Editor: Eben Muse

Eben Muse is Senior Lecturer in Digital Media at Bangor University and co-Director of the Stephen Colclough Centre for the History and Culture of the Book. He studies the impact of digital technologies on the cultural and commercial space of bookselling, and he is part-owner of a used bookstore in the United States.

ELEMENTS IN THE GATHERING

A full series listing is available at: www.cambridge.org/EPBC

Printed in the United States
by Baker & Taylor Publisher Services